THE ACCIDENTAL LAWYER

The Life and Times of Ted Salveter III

Ted Salveter

Bloomington, IN   Milton Keynes, UK

authorHOUSE™

AuthorHouse™
1663 Liberty Drive, Suite 200
Bloomington, IN 47403
www.authorhouse.com
Phone: 1-800-839-8640

AuthorHouse™ UK Ltd.
500 Avebury Boulevard
Central Milton Keynes, MK9 2BE
www.authorhouse.co.uk
Phone: 08001974150

First published by AuthorHouse   8/29/2006

ISBN: 1-4259-2819-6 (sc)

Printed in the United States of America
Bloomington, Indiana

This book is printed on acid-free paper.

Contents

FOREWARD

For several years I have wanted to write a book about my life. Why you ask do we need another book? Well, we probably don't, but this one is unique because it is about me. I guarantee you that no one else will write one about me. So if it is going to get done, I have to do it. I would have been eternally grateful to any of my ancestors who would have taken the time to shed a little light on who they were for the rest of us. None did. At the ripe old age of 69 I'm not sure who I am. Of course it doesn't really matter who I am. One can only stand so much navel gazing, especially someone else's navel. Like a lot of people, I still don't know what I want to be when I grow up. That isn't exactly true. I want to be better than Tiger Woods, and make a gazillion dollars. I am open to suggestions on how to do that, and don't give me that stuff about practicing. I hear enough of that from the pro.

The honest truth is that when you get older it really doesn't matter so much. I think I am learning that, but some days I think it does matter, and those are not my best days. My mom used to say that "you just had to know the truth and you would be in your rightful place". I hope this is it. That is probably what does matter. To be in your rightful place. Good luck on doing that. Maybe we'll know it when we get there.

I am quite sure that the readership of this book, if any, will be very limited. I realize that I may be the only one interested. That's okay. I would hope that some day my own children would read it and in so doing, have a better understanding of their father. Of course this is impossible for Tony, but I think he knew me pretty well anyway. Having never written an autobiography before I am not sure how to go about it. My life is connected to world events. Not that my life helped shape or change them in any way, but I know they contributed in making me who I am. I grew up in the 1940s and 50s. I really believe that these were terrific times to be a kid and student. Of course my family, friends and significant others will receive their due. Fairly or unfairly they are partly responsible for how I turned out.

I regret that so many people have passed away - most of my best resources have gone on. My mother, father, son, aunts, uncles, grandparents - most gone. With them their secrets and remembrances. I have tried not to include too many details and boring facts, but for the record to be complete, some are necessary.

I actually started this many years ago. Writing this book has forced me to recall a lot of things that had been long since locked away. This is not some tabloid tell all. It is strangely embarrassing that there isn't much to tell. Richie Cunningham and I have a lot in common. "Happy Days" is incredibly accurate regarding the teenage mindset in the 50s. Many, like my friend John Lewis, have asked who I thought would want to read this book? I have no idea. I guess that you do because you have read this far. Here it is, ready or not!

TED SALVETER, III

January, 2005

CHAPTER ONE

•Anticipation•

The team bus rocked along 67 highway from St. Louis to Alton, Illinois. It was a beautiful Fall Saturday morning in 1950. Western Military Academy was waiting for us. We were ready for them. I was 14 and a Freshman at The Principia. We were affectionately called "Haden's Cutthroats" after our captain Haden Edwards. Western was a rival in the ABC League. Nothing gets your blood pumping like the anticipation of a football game. I was prepared to hit somebody. I was ready.

Coach Phil Edwards was also my English teacher. He was working us up. Western wouldn't know what hit them. The dining hall had made our box lunches for after the game. There was one extra. Coach said it went to the "man" who made the first tackle. I knew it was mine. They won the toss and elected to receive. The kickoff sailed high into the air. The returner waited under the ball. I charged down the field like a raging bull, my eyes narrowed and focused on the ball carrier. I savored the lunch. He didn't have a chance. I creamed him. The extra lunch went to the bus driver. I don't remember being charitable.

Elation and disappointment. Good news, bad news. The story of my and probably everyone's life. I made the tackle, I didn't get the lunch. To be perfectly honest, mine has been a pretty good life. There's a lot of it I would do over again and a lot I'd do differently. Most of it I don't remember at all. Wouldn't it be great to have total recall? Maybe. Most of us don't. That's why they invented diaries. I don't have one.

I am 69 and now on Social Security. Who would have thought that would ever happen? I am trying to anticipate what life is going to be like from here on out. Admittedly most of my thoughts aren't positive. I do feel some urgency to see this through and I actually look forward to the process. It may be fun. Whoever you are reading this, you are probably someone I love or care a great deal about. I may still be here or I may be gone. Either way, I hope that you will bear with me and maybe get to know me better than you thought you did. I hope we'll still be friends. If I make a mistake be assured it is an honest one. I want to get it right.

CHAPTER TWO

•Sports•

A good part of my life has been devoted to playing sports and participating in athletics. I wish I could say that I had attained super star status, but I can't. I probably wasn't as good as I think I was. I'm convinced I could have been a lot better than I was. We all want to be the hero and win the big game. For guys, this is why "Damn Yankees" is such a popular musical. Who wouldn't sell his soul to the Devil for that one glorious season?

My Dad was a jock. He fully intended that his boys would be too. It seemed to take on me and my little brother Bob. Although brother Charles flirted with sports until he started college, he never seemed that interested. Charles was a good wrestler for Webster, and Bob played basketball for Ozark High School. Surprisingly my mother referred to Charlie as the "natural athlete" of the family. I used to think she meant it, but was it a little tongue in cheek? I never asked her directly. Nobody ever accused me of being a natural athlete, or a natural anything. Charlie may be the natural athlete. I've had to work hard for whatever I've accomplished.

Since I was 5 years older than Charles, I caught Dad closer to his prime and when he was still into it. Dad had been a star high school athlete at Webster Groves, especially in football and baseball. He graduated in 1929 and went to Missouri on a football scholarship. He played right tackle. Except in his later years, when he began to shrink and got sick, Dad was a lot bigger than me. He was 5'11" and 235 lbs. in his prime. Very big back in those days. At Webster his nickname was "Hippo".

I learned early on that I was no match for the Hippo and when he taught me how to block and tackle it was not a pretty sight. I usually ended up on my butt. Dad wasn't just big. He was fast and very coordinated. He could throw, kick and catch, and he was determined that I would too. He pretty much succeeded. Even though I wasn't a star I've been pretty good at all I've tried. All that banging around with a guy twice my size made me pretty tough too.

Dad insisted on toughness. No sissies allowed. Boys had to learn to fight. He taught me how to box. How to punch and how to duck. It came in pretty handy as the years went by. I don't know that I would recommend his methods. He had little patience, and I shed many a tear trying to get it right. I remember my Mom watching us from the screened in porch at the house at 548 Summit in Webster. Sometimes she would insist he stop or let up. I "threw like a girl" he'd say. There are no less kind words. I learned how to throw like a man. So did my boys.

Globe Democrat picture of father in 1929-football

Football

Football was the big sport as I grew up. I don't really remember playing it with other guys until we moved to Webster when I was in third grade at Lockwood School. This was 1944. They called it "sandlot" football back then. Nothing was organized like it is now.

No Mighty-Mites. It seems that everyday after school there was a game somewhere. We played at different places. Sometimes it was almost like neighborhood teams. There was a core of regulars with different guys mixed in depending on where we played. This stuff got pretty serious and there were lots of arguments and fights. The two places we played the most were Billy Foster's side yard at the corner of Greely and Caroline, and the Methodist Church at Greely and Bompart.

Nobody had uniforms and there was an array of helmets and shoulder pads. My dad (tight as he was) actually bought me a cheap pair of shoulder pads, pants and pretty much a cardboard helmet. I thought they were great. A lot of guys had nothing. Imagine hard hitting tackle football with no protection at all. Nobody ever got seriously hurt that I recall.

Some of the guys who played in those games were Billy Foster, John Loomis, Dick Bell, Dick Mann, Edgar Smith, Warren Bergman, Jack Soper, Tom Wilkinson and a host of others. There was a disparity in size, speed, age and ability. Even though it was sandlot, when you made a tackle, caught a pass or ran for a touch down it was a thrill and a big deal. I'm sure all those hours spent in the dirt, cold and mud helped develop much of the character I have today. Sometimes the guy who owned the football would get mad and threaten to go home. Negotiating skills were honed, but when all else failed we just threatened to beat him up if he left with the ball.

There was no school football in Webster until high school. However, for junior high (7th and 8th grades) there were service club teams in the St. Louis area. My first organized football team was in 7th grade on the Kiwanis Wildcats. This was the Webster team. Our coach was Charles J. Scullin. All I remember is that he seemed very old and was a wonderful and kind man. He also knew his football. I don't recall any of the Dads giving him any lip. (Dads always have advice for the coach). We were a pretty good team and won the league when I was in 8th grade. We got our picture in the St. Louis Post Dispatch and that was a big deal. This would have been in 1949. Our home games were played on the practice fields behind the high school on Saturday mornings. We probably practiced a couple of times a week.

Of all the memories I have from the Wildcats the most outstanding one was of the game with black players in it. Until then I had never played against a black. They had a back that was very fast and shifty. I was playing safety and from that defensive position behind everybody else you can see the whole field. He got the ball on a sweep around their left side. Our end was blocked out. The linebackers and others chased and missed. I moved up to my right. He got by our defensive half backs and suddenly it was just him and me. I would succeed where all the others had failed. I could hear the spectators screaming.

He was coming right at me. I was going to nail him for sure. I put my head down, lowered my shoulder and dove for his knees, ready to take him down and wrap my arms around his legs for a perfect tackle. The next thing I knew I was face down in the dirt with an arm full of air. He put a great move on me and I came up with only a glancing blow, with nothing. I looked back over my shoulder and saw him all alone, crossing the goal line. I glanced to the sidelines and saw the looks of disbelief and disappointment from our side. Of course, on their side they were jiving. I felt so exposed, so vulnerable, so much a failure. There was no place to hide. An experience like that can be pretty devastating, but one of the good things about sports and football in particular was that I had to get up, swallow my pride, and keep playing. I have to believe that I survived some of the later knockdowns of life because I learned that you don't quit. If you get pounded by the opponent or life you just get up and go until you get flattened again. It hurts, but it's the best way. After my son Tony was killed, this attitude and lesson learned early in life still gets me through many a rough day.

Principia is a prep school in St. Louis for Christian Scientists. We belonged to the Christian Science church in Webster on Selma Avenue. When I was in 8th grade at Webster Junior Hi, I was invited, along with other "Science" kids, to visit the campus at Page and Belt. I spent the day with 8th graders at Prin in class, lunch and all their activities. Now of course the reason for this visit was to try to get local kids to enroll in Principia. It is primarily a boarding school for students from all over the United States.

Near the end of the day they took us to the high school gym where we shot baskets and finally played a game. Several of the high school coaches were observing this. Even though football was my favorite sport, I was a pretty good basketball player and played on the Methodist basketball team. We also had organized intramural teams after school at Webster and the neighborhood games with hoops on people's garages. I remember playing pretty well that day, so well that some of the coaches were impressed and wanted me at Prin.

Principia was an expensive private school and we were pretty poor. My parents couldn't afford to send me. Somehow a mysterious benefactor came forth and paid my way. I started high school at Principia. Instead of playing football with all my buddies at Webster I was at a new school going to downtown St. Louis on the public bus every day.

That gets me back to Haden's Cutthroats. I played end on that team. In the Western game where I made the first tackle I also caught the winning touchdown pass. During the football banquet at the end of the season, as I was coming forward to get my letter, Coach Edwards told the crowd assembled that as slow as I was he still didn't know how I got behind their safety to catch that pass. I was pretty embarrassed and red faced by that remark. The truth is I don't know how I did it either. Though not slow, I wasn't blessed with blazing speed at that age, but I had good hands and a good sense of timing. Maybe I was just lucky.

That was a fun season and I loved Prin. Coach Edwards was a good athlete, and of course a lot bigger than his freshman charges. Lots of times he would get involved in our practices and personally run the ball or the play. When he did that we were more than welcome to try and tackle him. So one day there he was in his baseball cap, T-shirt and football pants, demonstrating an end around. Nobody had ever laid a hand on him before, but that day I nailed him good. There was a gasp from the team, and as we both laid there on the ground I thought that I was dead meat. What had I been thinking of? He glared at me. The team held its breath, I looked for a hole to crawl in. Then he broke into a big grin and said "Nice tackle Salveter". We all breathed a collective sigh of relief. I had done the impossible and lived!

My Dad in many ways was not the ideal father. He and Mom divorced that year (1951). It was his fault. Divorce was pretty rare back then, and it meant that it was back to public school for me. In 10th grade I made the cuts and played at Webster for old coach Frobel Gaines. "Froggy", as others called him, had actually been my Dad's baseball coach at Webster. Dad somehow made it to almost all of my football games. He didn't sit in the stands either. Nope, Dad would prowl the sidelines right on the line of scrimmage. There were two adults yelling orders at me at all times. One was Dad and the other was my coach. Sometimes that got pretty confusing. He was tough on me but he was my biggest fan too. I'm sure that I had a lot of mixed emotions about him being there and so vocal. Adolescents are easily confused and embarrassed. But there is no doubt that now I am happy that he got to see me play and that he cared. He died at 86 in July of 1995. Up to his death we still talked a lot about football. It was a bond we had for life.

Froggy had a great football record. Webster's sophomore team ("B" team) almost always won the Suburban League. You would think that when all that talent got to the Varsity, Webster would be unbeatable. We won the Suburban League that year, 1951, and I think that we were undefeated. The problem was that Froggy didn't spend much time on the basics like blocking and tackling. We spent most of our practices learning trick plays. For instance Charlie Dring was a huge tackle and could throw the ball 70 yards. We had a razzle-dazzle play where the ball would end up hidden on the ground. He would pick it up and heave it downfield to a wide open receiver.

Those tricks worked great against other 10th graders, but for some reason they weren't very effective at the Varsity level when a more basic brand of football was played. Coach Ray Moss was always amazed at how much time he had to spend with the juniors on the fundamentals. "Damn Froggy and his trick plays". Froggy's trick plays and unbelievable records were always making Coach Moss look bad. How could he screw up such talented players?

Coach Gaines made a center out of me. One of the things that Dad had taught me at an early age was to center the ball. It's not easy. It's a backward pass between your legs. Ever remember seeing a pro center the ball over the back or kicker's head? I can tell you that nothing memorable or exciting happens when you are the center. It's all a big blur, "trench warfare". I never did like having to look back between my legs knowing that the defender across from me, who I couldn't look at, was going to try to take my head off. It wasn't as bad when the quarterback was over center in the T formation. Then you could look at the sucker and growl back at him, but you still had to get the darn ball snapped before you could do anything. I took a beating at center, but I never made a bad snap or threw it over anybody's head.

Once in a while we would run a trick play where the quarterback would give the ball back to me and I would run it. I never ran it very far. All of Froggy's trick plays didn't work. I think that play is illegal now. I guess we learned some defense too because we outscored our opponents 215-12 that year. We had 3 shutouts and beat Normandy 47-0.

Varsity football at Webster was a big deal. My junior year started with high anxiety. There were only so many places on the team and obviously everyone on the "B" team wouldn't make it. Webster was a big 4A school and lots of people tried out. Lots of people would get "cut". The process was that tryouts and practice were held in August before school started. August in St. Louis is unbelievably hot and humid. Practices were brutal. Twice a day, 8 a.m. to 10 a.m. and 3 p.m. to 5 p.m. After the first week the cuts start. A list is posted outside the coach's office of those guys who made the cut and who should come back the next day. Each day a new list is posted until the team roster is complete. I can tell you that there were plenty of anxious faces each day looking at that list. There were also a few tears from some who didn't make it. No wonder they didn't make it! Football players that cry? I don't know if I would have cried or not because I made it.   They made a guard out of me that year. Well at least it was better than center. Of course I wasn't first string, but I was close so I got to play pretty much. Guard is another one of those positions where all the action seems pretty much the same. It's mean and dirty down in those trenches. I didn't care - I loved every minute of it. I couldn't wait for school to get out so we could get to practice.

We had a pretty good team in 1952 but we didn't win the Suburban League. The schools were Webster, Kirkwood, Maplewood, University

City, Ritneour, Normandy, Clayton and Brentwood. We had 3 wins, 3 losses and 3 ties that year. It was a big come down for we juniors who the year before had annihilated the competition.

I don't remember the first football game that I actually watched. We had no TV then, and unlike today we were not bombarded with sports news. I didn't read the newspapers, so the football and other sports I knew was for the most part limited to Webster. I'm sure that the first game I saw would have been a Webster Hi game and more than likely the "Turkey-Day" game against Kirkwood.

In Webster, on Thanksgiving Day, football and turkey went hand in hand. The big bird had to wait until the game was over. Football started in Webster in 1903. 1907 was the first game with Kirkwood. The winner gets the Frisco Bell, the loser the Little Brown Jug. It's still that way today. On Thanksgiving Day 1952 I played in my first and only Turkey Day game. What a thrill. We hated Kirkwood with a passion. The night before I got in a fight with Kirkwood students when we raided their bon-fire. In 1939 they didn't play because of fights. It was a very cold day with a little snow on the ground. Neither team could generate much offense and it was scoreless late in the game. Kirkwood had a very fast back by the name of Pete Van Dam. He got loose on a long run around left end. He had run 50 yards and appeared headed for the winning touchdown. We were sick. No one would ever catch him, especially me. I was at least 20 yards behind.

But out of the blue Hank Kuhlman did catch him on about our 20 yard line. They never scored and the game ended a scoreless tie. I never thought I would be happy with a tie, but I was. The traditional Thanksgiving meal at my aunt Helen's was great.

Hank Kuhlman was only a sophomore then. When he was a senior he led Webster to the 4-A State Championship, and an undefeated season. He was all Big 8 at Missouri and even played some pro ball. He coached at Missouri under Dan Devine, and coached in the NFL at Green Bay, Chicago, Indianapolis and Arizona. Hank would tell you that he still remembers that tackle in 1952.

About 40 years after that 1952 season I was talking with one of my brother Charles' good friends, Don Bracy of Ozark, Missouri. Don is a very successful real estate developer, and I had actually known him for many years. We are the same age, and when he said he grew up in Quincy, Illinois, I asked him if he played football. He had. Turns out we played against each other when Webster traveled to Quincy. I remembered that game as the roughest I ever played in. There was a lot of blood, and a lot of our guys carried off. They beat us 20-6, but it seemed like 100-6. Quincy is a strange place to go for your big road game. The team stayed in a small hotel there after our night game drubbing. It's a small world.

During practice one day I got kicked in the face, and a tooth on the lower left side got knocked out. I still have the same partial that old Doc Campbell put in for me.

My senior year at Webster in 1953 started with those dreaded August tryouts. There was no anxiety about making the cuts and making the team now. The challenge was to be first string. The competition was pretty stiff. I still figured that I'd be playing guard. In addition to being older, I was stronger and a lot bigger. As a freshman I was 120 pounds, sophomore 145, junior 160, but now I had reached what would turn out to be my full growth, 5' 11" and 180 pounds. I've stayed there ever since, except I am getting shorter, just like my Dad. I hate that. I also discovered that I was a lot faster and instead of lagging behind in the wind sprint races I was right there near the front.

The two a days were as tough as ever, but what I realized is that I was dishing out a lot more than I was taking. One on one blocking and tackling drills were a chance to knock somebody on their butt and impress the coach. Our line coach was "Bear" Bryant. He seemed to love my hard hitting aggressiveness. In two weeks I had nailed down the starting right guard spot on both offense and defense. This was going to be a great senior year.

But something happened to change all that. One of those watershed moments in your life. I got a call from the head coach at Principia wanting me to come back there for my senior year. Whitey Schubert was a pretty persuasive guy. I had to make a decision, and make it quick. I didn't know what to do. I was set at Webster. I liked Principia and knew I could play there too. There was a lot of prayer by Mom and me as to what to do. I felt like a yo-yo bouncing back and forth between the two schools.

I still couldn't afford to go to Prin but again an anonymous donor had made it possible for me to have a full scholarship. I never found out who it was. Webster was a pretty rich town. We were poor. We had no car. Dating was a nightmare without one. Keeping up financially with my "Socie" friends was a problem. Prin was a rich prep school but no one was allowed to have a car and money didn't mean much. The campus life was a great equalizer. You made it on what you could do and not who you were. That turned out not to be totally true as we'll see later. It's never true anywhere or in anything in life.

The decision was made that I would go to Principia. I went to practice the next morning as usual, but I didn't dress out. All the guys were getting on their pads, but I just nervously talked to them. Finally Coach Moss came into the locker room joking with the guys as he came through. Then he saw I wasn't dressed and asked if I was sick or something. I told him that I needed to talk to him so we went into his office. I explained the situation, hoping that he would be understanding. He wasn't. He blew his top. Threatened to report me and Principia to the Missouri Athletic Association for giving and accepting scholarships or money to high school athletes. He got pretty loud and pounded his desk a lot.

When I left his office all the guys were staring at me and very quiet. I felt like Benedict Arnold. I cleaned out my locker, turned in my uniform, said goodbye to everyone and went home. I was pretty sure that I had really screwed up.

I didn't have long to think about it because Prin was starting its pre-school practice that day. I had to pack to go away because football camp was held at the Principia College Campus at Elsah, Illinois. I would be living in Buck House, one of the men's dorms, for the next two weeks. August on the river at Elsah wasn't any cooler than August in Webster. I was getting a double dose of football. A whole new round of two a days was to begin.

The campus at Elsah is gorgeous, but it was sort of like being in prison. Coach Schubert had us under his thumb all day and night. I was in pretty good shape by now so it was easier for me but it wasn't easy. Schubert was tough as hell, and a few of the guys just couldn't handle it. His methods were always a subject of debate and criticism. Given my nature, I kind of liked it and accepted the challenge. In addition to the two a days we had chalk talks in the evenings. I had no trouble sleeping.

We ate all our meals at the college cafeteria. There was a tradition that Dr. Happ, who taught at the college, would invite a few guys over for breakfast one day before practice. His son, George, was in my class, and was the team manager. George liked me, and I guess that's why I got asked to go. The breakfast was great, especially the fresh blueberry muffins that Mrs. Happ made. I sort of overdid it on the muffins and everything in general, somehow forgetting that shortly I'd be out there in the hot sun for the first practice of the day. Needless to say, after a few wind sprints, duck walks and other drills, the muffins were no longer with me. They weren't nearly as good coming up as they were going down.

A few of the college players worked out with us. That was a challenge. Especially with Matt Stitt who was a legend in his own time. For some odd reason we practiced in these old leather helmets instead of the new plastic "bubble helmets". They were saving them for the games. That all changed when I crushed one and got knocked out. From then on we always practiced in the good helmets.

Football camp was finally over, and we headed back to St. Louis to start school. The rest of the students were arriving when we pulled onto the campus. Of course, we thought we were pretty hot stuff, and got the appropriate admiring looks from girls and boys alike.

The good thing about football at Prin was that I was no longer a center or a guard. I was now a linebacker and halfback. I liked that much better. I was a starter on defense, and I also received all the kickoffs and punts. I felt I should be a starter on offense too but that would have benched a guy who had started the year before. This is where the politics began to start, but I wasn't entirely aware of it at the time.

Earl P. "Whitey" Schubert is an unforgettable character. He will always be my "coach" and my friend. It was not love at first sight. As I indicated earlier, he had some controversial methods that had raised the hackles of some at Principia for years. You either loved or hated the guy. I can't remember all of the things that we had to do, but these are some of them.

We did not play our games at the school. We played our home games in Overland at Taylor Field. Sometimes we practiced there too. This meant dressing out at school and riding the bus each day west on Page to Taylor Field. It was a mile from Page and Walton Road to Taylor Field. If we had lost the game on Saturday, then on Monday the bus would stop and we'd run the mile to the field in full gear. This was affectionately known as "Schubert's Mile". Always looking for ways to beat the system I remember lagging behind, waiting for the bus and coach to go on, and flagging down a car. I laid down in the back seat as we passed the guys so they wouldn't see me. I had him let me out before we got to the field. I had outsmarted the old man. Unfortunately coach had the bus driver let him out of the bus before the field too and was hiding behind a tree. He saw what I did. He congratulated me on getting to the field first and then had me run

1.5 miles on the track.

The "Bear Pit" was probably the cruelest thing we did. Everyone would stand in a circle and coach would call out two numbers. Those two guys had to fight it out in the middle of the circle. Having had a few fights, this didn't bother me so much but for some of the guys it was shear terror. It was sort of kill or be killed. It was over once you had your opponent down. It wasn't as bad as it looked, but it was bad. First of all everyone had football gear on, so you couldn't get hurt too much unless someone landed a good shot in an unprotected place. It was more the idea of it. To outsiders it seemed barbaric. Coach actually did a pretty good job of making some men out of boys.

The "funnel" was fun too. The tackler waited at one end, and the ball carrier ran straight at him. Neither could try to avoid the other. It was my luck to tackle Vern Hannesen our 6'5" 330 pound tackle from Winnipeg, Canada a few times.

The "Duck Walk" was great. You simply duck walked from one end of the field back to where you started. Sometimes it was done as a race, so if you lost you got to do it again.

There were all of the regular tackling and blocking drills, wind sprints etc. Coach finally gave up the mandatory boxing matches when some of the mothers went berserk. He had been a boxer for the University of Maryland, so that was dear to his heart. That explains why we always sang the Maryland fight song and anthem on the bus. Carl Osterloh had graduated from Prin a year ahead of me and went on to play football and baseball for Missouri. He was afraid that being from a small private school he wouldn't be able to handle big time football drills. In his four years at Mizzou he never had any practices even close to being as tough as Schubert's practices.

We weren't ready for our first game against Brentwood. I was eager to play them because they were in the Suburban League. We couldn't execute, killed ourselves with fumbles, and lost the opener 6-0. That was a wake up call. We won our next game against Louisiana, Missouri. Coach sent in a play. We were supposed to kick a field goal. We were pretty far out for a field goal so the quarterback called a play for me to run up the middle to get closer and more in the center of the field. The problem was that I made one of the best runs of my life and zig- zagged about 35 yards for a touchdown. I was thrilled when I came off the field as they were kicking the extra point. Coach was furious with me for not following his orders and going for the field goal.

Then we walloped Wellston. I was very aggressive that day - too aggressive. One of their backs drove up the middle. I was playing linebacker. He was pretty much stopped by our line but I hit him pretty hard anyway. He hurt his neck and had to be carried off to the hospital in an ambulance. No penalty was called on me, but I knew that I had been wrong. I was so sick to my stomach as they attended to him and carried him off that I thought I would throw up. I'm not totally sure what happened to him, but I think it was pretty bad. I learned a big lesson, and have never ever really gotten over it.

Later in that game I ran back a punt and was tackled and knocked out of bounds. The guy who tackled me wouldn't let go and stayed on top of me. I got mad and hit him with the ball. He still didn't let go and I slugged him. I was out of the game. Officials won't stand for that.

We opened the ABC League against Western Military and beat them pretty bad. I remember running off of right tackle, smacking right into two huge linemen, spinning and cutting to the outside and scoring from about 20 yards out.

Country Day was always tough and state ranked. My old classmate from Lockwood and junior high, Edgar Smith, played end for them. Even though we only lived a few blocks apart I never saw him anymore. It was good to briefly visit before we "laced 'em up". They won the ABC League and had two All State players, Trigg and Disbro, on their team. At Webster we never got scouting reports, although the coaches did scout and clued us in. At Prin, we got written scouting reports that were usually right on the money. Trigg was very fast, about 6' and a 200 pound back. Disbro was about a 6'4" end, and very hard to cover. As linebacker I had to key a lot on what their left guard did to start a play. One play we were to particularly look out for was Trigg getting a pitch from the quarterback that looked like an end run but if the pulling guard did something (I can't remember what now) then look out for Trigg, who was left handed, throwing a half back pass to Disbro. I saw the guard do it but it registered too late. I moved over to take the run and forgot to stay with Disbro. I had that sick feeling when I saw the pass sail over my head and into a wide open Disbro's hands. The score was 7-0 pretty quick.

I loved to tackle and never flinched except once. The "Codaso" game was not my finest. Their field was mostly dirt and like playing on concrete. I caught Trigg breaking to his right past our line and at full speed. For the first time I hesitated. Frozen momentarily in fear. I only got a small piece of him as he went by for a big gain. It was 19-0 at the half. We had all played terrible. The second half was different. We won it but lost the game 19-6. I caught a pass for our only score. I was so furious with myself that I played possessed the second half. I relished every chance I had to hit Trigg. They didn't score again. It was some sort of moral victory.

Next we ran over Lutheran 38-0 and then went to Chicago for our big road trip. We played Elgin Academy. When you are the team from out of town you can try to act like the conquering heroes. When we pulled onto their campus, still in our street clothes, we decided to use one of our intimidation tactics. We had some big guys on the team. I already mentioned Vern Hanneson. We would be sure that all the biggest guys got off the bus first to try and scare the opponents. I remember one of their cheerleaders saying, "please don't hurt our guys!" Actually we hurt them pretty bad and won 42-7. It got so bad that nobody was playing their normal position. I even got to quarterback for a while. I don't know why I remember so many goofy things I did, but in that game I broke through the middle of the line and started up field. It was like a textbook demonstration of running and stiff arming would be tacklers. You run with the ball securely tucked in your arm pit and the cup of your hand. You hold tight to avoid fumbling even if hit. If you have the ball in your right hand and the tackler is on that side, then you must quickly shift the ball to your left hand. This can be a lot of shifting back and forth if they are coming from all sides. A tackle to the right, shift to left hand, stiff arm with right. Tackler to the left - well you know the procedure. I was shifting right and left and bowling over tacklers with crushing stiff arms. I was going to score. The problem was that on one of those stiff arms I forgot to shift and I was merrily running down the field without the ball. Very embarrassing.

One of the traditions at Prin was to have a practice at the school outside the Big Gym. It was the old football field and then the soccer field. Tom Clark was our fullback. His Dad, Burt, was a little guy, not over 140 pounds. He had been a great player for Missouri. One of the guys explained what was going to happen. Mr. Clark was going to be by himself at one end of the field. The first string would kick off and he would run the ball through us. No blockers, no interference. It was 11-1. I said "you've got to be kidding. We'll crunch the old guy". Mr. Clark passed on well into his 90s. He would have been 45 to 48 years old at the time. He looked really old to me. I decided that I personally would set him on his can. He also was wearing only football shoes, football pants and a T-shirt. We lined up. I looked down the field. He looked so small and helpless all alone waiting for the ball. We had no strategy. My strategy was to just nail him and end this silly tradition. The whistle blew, the kick sailed in the air. He waited, he caught it and he started at us. We charged at him. I'll never know what went through Burt Clark's mind, but he had to know I or someone was going to pulverize him. Maybe so, but it wasn't going to be that day. Nobody laid a hand on him. I missed by two feet. How embarrassing. Now that I am old I really admire what he did and have taken every opportunity in my life to show up the younger generation.

My football career came to an end on a beautiful November Day at Taylor Field. When you are a senior playing in your last game it can be pretty traumatic. You want to savor every minute of it. We played John Burroughs, one of our rivals, and a team Prin may have never beaten before. It seems like I remember every minute of that game. A sad note was that Coach Schubert's father had died, and he had to fly back to Maryland. I wanted him there for our last game.

I remember several things in that game. In the first half I made a "spear tackle" and knocked myself out. I was lucky I didn't break my neck. I remember coming to, flat on my back and seeing all of our team standing over me in a circle. The crowd was quiet. I could actually hear my girlfriend crying in the stands. I insisted I was okay. There was no way I was going to miss that game. I remember being down and looking at my left hand that was flat on the ground in front of me. Suddenly a huge cleated football shoe crunched it. I figured it was broken. It was pretty bloody. They taped it up and I went back into the game.

In the second half the game was tied 6-6. They threw a short pass over the middle and I intercepted it in a crowd. I have had several occasions in athletics where I seemed to go berserk and gain super strength. This was one of them. By all rights I should have been tackled on the spot but I refused to be. I knocked tacklers over like they were straw and started running toward their goal. I intercepted on about our 35 yard line so I had 65 yards to go to score the winning touchdown. I was possessed. I ran over and around everybody and down the left sideline. Two yards from the end zone someone caught me from behind, and knocked me out of bounds. I had almost made it. I was a hero anyway as I came off the field. We had the ball, first down on their 2 yard line. We couldn't fail to score.

We did fail to score. Our fullback fumbled on the very first play and they got it back. Someone came out of the stands and insisted that I play in the backfield the rest of the game since he was having a terrible day, and I did seem to be up for it. I don't know what Coach Schubert would have done but politics kept him in the game and me on defense. I don't know if it would have made any difference but it couldn't have hurt. The game ended in a 6-6 tie. Not the way I wanted to go out.

I could have tried to play in some small college somewhere and I wish I had. My football scholarship to Principia College was withdrawn because of my bad grades. I played "flag" football at Drury for my fraternity. That was pretty tough and a lot of fun, but I missed the daily practices and the games. After that there were lots of touch football games in law school and after, but my real football career was over that day in 1953.

1953 Country Day v. Principia

1952 Webster Groves Ted 3rd Row 2nd from right

1953 Principia Ted No. 48

1950 Principia Ted No. 17

Grace, Timmermans, Hohenemser, O'Kelley, Dring, Fitzgerald, Von Hoffmann, Elster, Odot, Thomas, Porter, Marsh, Brendecke, Loomis, DeLong, Schwartz, Carr, Mueller, Cliff, Coach Gaines, Knickman, Hellmick, Whyte, Carothers, Stauber, Love, Zeis, Salveter, Heineman, Stauber, Schwartz, Brown, Mueller, Toft, Greene, Bickel.

1951

BASKETBALL

Since Dad wasn't particularly interested in basketball my interest was not as great as in football. There was a basket at John Loomis' house and we played on dirt. It was okay except when it got the slightest bit wet. The dirt would get so ingrained in your hands it was almost impossible to get out. The ball would eventually be caked in mud. It seemed good enough to us. Dick Bell had a goal on his garage (single car) so the playing surface of concrete was better. It was pretty narrow and it sloped down to the street. A drive to the basket was uphill. Sometimes we could get in the small gym at the Baptist Church on Summit. We also figured out a way to break in through the roof. Occasionally we would sneak through the skylight into the gym at the high school, and the old YMCA on Lockwood had an outdoor court behind it.

The facilities would not favorably compare to what kids have available today, but we had fun none-the-less. There were no Y or other leagues in St. Louis. Nothing much until you started high school. In junior high I did play for the Methodist Church in a church league and an intramural team at school. To play for the Methodists I had to go to their church. This was tough since I went to the Christian Science Church. You had to go at least 50% of the time. So on 2 Sundays a month I would first go to the Methodist

Sunday School and then walk over to the Christian Science Sunday
School which started an hour later. I used to get into a few interesting
theological debates with my poor Methodist teacher.

We used to play "football-basketball", a game I guess we invented.
There were no fouls. You tried to score, but the defender could do
what he wanted to stop you. It got pretty rough, and there were lots
of fights. It wasn't particularly good training for real basketball where
the object is not to foul. However, it certainly prepared me to play
pick up games or "Y Ball" later in life.

I played on the Freshman team at Principia. The "C" team as they
called it in the ABC League. Perhaps I should explain the concept of
the league which exists no where else to my knowledge. In football
there were weight limits to "C" and "B" teams, but no limits to the
"A" team. This helped eliminate some of the great size disparities
and potential injuries of mismatched younger players. I guess there
were height limits in basketball. It's a good idea but nobody else does
it. I think that our "C" team was probably pretty bad and the scores
were ridiculously low. Defense was emphasized, and because there
was no organized youth basketball like today (starts at age 5 now)
the dribbling and scoring skills were not as advanced as today. We
also didn't have TV to watch college and pro players, so there were
no "Michael Jordan moves" to emulate. It really was a time of great
innocence in a lot of ways. The only notoriety I got in the school year

book described a game against Western that we lost 19-16. It simply said "Salveter was the steadiest shot and ball handler". Maybe so.

I don't even remember going out for basketball at Webster. Football lasted so late and basketball practices started before we were through. Besides, the basketball situation at Webster was real clique, and I had messed up by not being there my Freshman year. I continued to play intramurals and anywhere else I could, but it was not a particularly big deal to me.

My senior year at Prin was a big deal, and when football was over I was ready to try out for the basketball team. A lot of guys who didn't play football had been working out all Fall. It's a hard transition to get your "football muscles" ready to play basketball. When we got them going, we produced the best team the school had ever had up to then and probably since. We won more games, scored more points, had the highest point per game average than any prior team and went to state. We won our first 7 games against some pretty good City schools.

I immediately ran into politics again in basketball. The guy who was the starting guard the prior year's father was a trustee. I could play rings around him and yet he started and I didn't. After a few games of out scoring and out playing him off the bench I went nuts and took things into my own hands. In practice the 1st five always scrimmaged the 2nd five. One day I decided to make the point the best I could. On defense I screamed at and harassed him and every other starter. On rebounds and scoring I went crazy. I made him look particularly bad by stealing balls, blocking shots, etc. To put it bluntly, I made a complete ass of myself. Coach Schubert was furious.

He called me into his office after practice and really chewed me out. He would not allow any disruptions in team harmony. I told him I understood, and having always been a team player it was not something I had wanted to do, but I felt I had no choice. I told him that he and I both knew I was better than the other fellow, and it was not fair to me to have him start. I was sure we would both do the right thing in the future. I'm sure that Coach was in a tough spot, and one coaches often find themselves in. I know that I was close to being off the team.

He did do the right thing and I started all the rest of the season. I not only started but I blossomed. (Remember that Michael Jordan got cut his first year) I became one of our leading scorers, and was high man in many games. Suddenly basketball was becoming pretty important to me. Coach even started devising plays to get me open for my jump shot. Scoring was fun and I loved it, but my football instincts caused me to play hard-nosed defense and I reveled in that. I simply would not back off or give up. I took it as a personal insult every time the other team scored. A lot of guys don't like to play defense. I believe that you play at both ends of the floor.

There were many highlights for me that year and I'll share a few I can remember. Bayless had a guy playing for them named Sonny Siebert. We played them twice that year. Sonny was a great athlete and became a professional baseball player. He was a solid pitcher in the majors for many years. He and I guarded each other in those two games and we had some real battles. I held my own against a really good player. I stood the test.

McKinley had an all state guard by the name of Nash. We had a great battle. I outscored him and fouled him out. I had a trick where I would look like I was loosely dribbling the ball and it would be easy to steal. It was a trap. When the defender would go for it I would pull it back and turn my body toward him so that he would usually foul me. Nash never figured it out. The more frustrated he got, the harder he tried to make me look bad, and the more he fouled. I hit a lot of free throws that year. Against Western I scored 12 points on free throws alone. Schubert preferred that old underhanded way, but I convinced him I was more effective the "modern way".

I don't remember who we were playing, but during a home game with all our students (girls) and faculty in the stands, a crazy thing happened. The other team had just scored, and Dave Lang (the other guard and brother of Hope Lang the movie star), and I were bringing the ball up court. We were just passing it back and forth when I heard a whistle blow to my left. There was an official over there, so I looked left to see why he blew the whistle. Just at that moment Lang threw the ball to me and it hit me in the head. The ball bounced into the hands of the guy guarding me, and he went in for an uncontested lay-up. Schubert was furious and immediately yanked me out of the game. He was yelling and screaming at me in front of everyone, and I was trying to explain that I heard a whistle. He wasn't buying it. Then the Principal came out of the stands and told coach he had heard a whistle too. A kid with a whistle was found and kicked out, and coach settled down. Soon I was back in the game. I learned not to take my eye off the ball for anything after that.

We took another trip to Chicago for our basketball road trip. We played Lutheran North on Friday night and Lutheran South on Saturday night. We won the Friday night game pretty easy in the smallest gym I ever played in. The Saturday night game was played in a very big gym and was very exciting. Coach benched me after I was whistled for allegedly tripping and making a comment. We were ahead when I went out, and with a couple of minutes to go he put me back in because we were behind. With about 30 seconds to go they were ahead by 1, had the ball, and just trying to run out the clock. They hadn't counted on me stripping the ball. Tom Buttner took off, and I hit him with a pass. He scored the lay-up with just a few seconds left, and we won by 1. All was forgiven about the alleged trip and comment.

We got into the districts or regionals or whatever they called them back then, and played an all black city school. This was a first for me, and probably everyone else. They started fast and completely dominated us. I had never seen the stuff they did with a basketball. Unbelievable passes, free style playing and improvising. It was "run and gun" at its best. I thought that we would lose 100-0. We took a time out to settle down. We were to play our deliberate offense and work our plays. We were to put a little more pressure on them defensively. Pretty soon those unbelievable passes started to go astray and those play ground shots stopped falling. It was the "Tortoise and the Hare" all over again. In the second half their game completely unraveled and we plodded on to victory. Still I was amazed by all that undisciplined talent.

We qualified to go to State. I'm not sure that any Prin team had ever done that before. We traveled to Troy Missouri and played Troy in the first round. That was a weird set up because the gym was a giant stage, and the fans actually sat out in the audience. Talk about your home town advantage! I don't know what happened to us that night but we played terrible. Troy was a run and gun team, and they hit from everywhere all night long. We couldn't really stop them and we couldn't catch up. It was a poor way for a great season to end.

Baseball started soon after, but basketball was not forgotten. Coach advised me that he had some interest in me from several schools, and that I might be getting some scholarship offers. This was a process that I was totally unfamiliar with. I can assure you that neither Kentucky or UCLA were interested. Eventually I had offers from Drury College, Washington University, Southeast Missouri, Missouri Valley and one other that I can't remember. The people at Drury seemed the most interested and I decided to take what they offered. Finances for college were definitely going to be a problem, and although Drury didn't offer a full scholarship, they did offer a partial one and a work grant. This, plus what I could make in the summer, would be enough. I was going to Springfield.

I didn't know it that Spring, but my basketball career was about over too. There were several guys in the Freshman Class on scholarship to Drury. They had us meet together as soon as we got to school. Many of them became friends right away like Noel Koelling from Maplewood, Lanny Benson from Sedalia and Larry Freund from Warsaw. At some point, after practice officially got started, I got in a disagreement with Coach Al Weiser about what was important in a basketball player and some other dumb stuff. To my constant regret ever since, I quit the team. I've made some stupid decisions in my life, but that one ranks right near the top. I can't give you a logical reason. It was a crazy 18 year-old's decision.

I didn't seek anyone's advice. My folks were divorced and Dad didn't even want me in college. I never got any advice from him. I figured that Mom wouldn't understand. I didn't even discuss it with Coach Schubert. Hell I didn't even discuss it with Coach Weiser or Coach Kanehl. It makes me sick to think about it. I did see Coach Schubert over Christmas break, and when I told him he was very upset with me. I didn't blame him. He had worked hard to get me the scholarship.

I was on the junior varsity until I quit. I should have at least waited until they took the team picture. I really liked Coach Kanehl, but never cared much for Weiser for a while. The JV games were pretty much an after thought. We played at odd times. There wasn't much fan support, at least not while I was there. Interestingly we played the Forsyth or Branson high school team one afternoon at Weiser Gym. They would win the State Championship that year. We beat them pretty bad. Thom Field was on that team, and although I didn't know him then, when we both became attorneys in Springfield we played together on the Lawyers' Basketball team.

I played on my fraternity basketball team at Drury and that was a lot of fun. When I started law school at St. Louis University, and discovered that we had some good players in our Freshman class, we formed a law school team (The Tortfeasors) and entered the inter-fraternity league. There was considerable complaining about our eligibility but they let us in. They also let the Dental School team in and for each of the 3 years I was in law school we played the Dental

School in the finals. We won 2 of the 3. Everybody on that team had played college ball somewhere. They all had better careers than me. John McCartney (St. Louis U), John King (St. Benedicts), Joe Teasdale (Rockhurst), Gus Luepke (Notre Dame) and John Hannegan (Central Missouri State).

While in law school I also played on my church team, Webster Baptist, and the Marine Reserve Team. Actually I played on the Marine Reserve team in Springfield when I was at Drury. One of my years in law school, I had such a good season that I was chosen to play on a St. Louis city All Star Team. We played against a semi-pro team as a warm up game before one of the St. Louis Hawk's games at Kiel Auditorium. That was a real thrill for me. We won that game but I fouled out. When the game was over, we were briefly on the floor with Easy Ed McCauley, Cliff Hagan and Bill Russell. They were playing the Celtics.

After I started practicing law in Springfield, Jim Prewitt and I started the Lawyers' Team. We were pretty good some years. Some of the guys who played in those years with me were Jim Prewitt, John Lewis, Thom Field, Duane Cox, Lindell Church, Dick Wilson, Kerry Montgomery, Hank Westbrooke, Jerry Estes, Tom Knapp, Don Jones (yes, Don Jones), Jerry Lowther and others. I also played on "church" teams at the Y in church leagues. It was all a lot of fun, and I still run into people I played against and fought with. When I was in the

Legislature from 1968-1971 we played some exhibition games, and worked out at Lincoln University in Jefferson City.

In the twilight of my career, when I was by far the oldest lawyer still playing, we started a series of annual games with the doctors. The games would be played at Drury and became a big deal. This was in the 1980's. We had an over 40 team and an under 40 team. Each played two quarters. The lawyers usually won, but Steve Grace and Dave Nelson pulled the "docs" through a few times. The purpose of the game was to have fun and raise money for the American Cancer Society. The doctors finally refused to play us anymore because Bob Stufflebaum was upset about malpractice and divorce lawyers. The games got pretty physical, and there were a few altercations (always started by the doctors).

When I was getting near 50 or about, I still played, and although I could still get up and down the floor, I didn't handle the blows and injuries too well. I decided to quit except for occasional pick up games at the Y, etc. One of my last games was when our Evangel Temple team played the CBC Varsity. We actually beat them, but I thought my lungs would burn out. I still shoot around now and then and even played at the Y some recently. After knee operations in 1989 and 1990 it's not a pretty sight. It's a game I highly recommend.

1950 Principia Ted No. 19

1953 Principia Ted No. 8

1962 Lawyers' Team. Front row, l to r: John Lewis, Jerry Estes, Jerry Lowther, Ted Salveter.

Back row, l to r: Duane Cox, Jim Prewitt, Lindell Church, Dick Wilson, Tom Knapp.

BASEBALL

As you can see by now, my autobiography would have been a lot shorter if I hadn't been an all around jock. My life seems to have been dominated by sports. I'm not complaining. I played on some little league teams in Webster like the Optimists or such, but it was nothing outstanding. On Laclede Station Road across from a bar called Cousin Hugos, there was a ball field. This was near our house, but I think it was in Maplewood and not Webster. I'm not sure. Anyway, we went down there to play baseball. A lot of times we would play "Indian Ball". It's a fun game. You have a home plate and about 100' or so, two markers which create the boundaries and a sort of V shaped field. You only need 4 guys to play. The infield is that area between the two markers. The outfield is all beyond that. You don't run bases. Your own team mate pitches you an easy ball to hit and you try to hit it by or over the infielders. If he catches a ground ball or a fly ball you are out. If the outfielder catches a fly you are out. Two foul balls on the same side and you are out. Everything else is a single unless you hit it over the outfielders which is a home run.

When we had enough guys we could play an actual game. Lots of times we would arrange to play guys who would come over from Maplewood. They were a pretty skuzzy lot, and we gave them their distance. Because of the Cardinals, with Stan Musiel and the others, we all fantasized that we would one day be big league players. We played other places too, such as Old Orchard behind Pevely Dairy or Eden Seminary or the High School. Anyplace. When I was a Freshman at Prin, I went out for the baseball team and actually made it with a few other Freshmen. We were like a farm club because there wasn't much chance we would ever get to play. We even got hand me down uniforms. That was probably a pretty good idea on Schubert's part because a few years later some of us were pretty good.

I was an outfielder. My uniform was too big and probably looked goofy. I remember actually getting in a game once at Taylor Field. He put me in center field. I felt like I had been swallowed up. There's no help near you in center. I was hoping that no one would hit me a ball, but someone did. It was a single right up the middle. The guy on second was trying to score. I actually fielded the ball perfectly and heaved it toward our catcher who was crouched and waiting at home plate. I was so excited and pumped up that I actually threw it over the back stop. Everybody scored.

Back at Webster I don't remember going out my sophomore year. I'm not sure that anyone did. My junior year I was going out but I got an infection in my foot that almost killed me and I was bed-ridden for weeks. I was so weak after that that I didn't perform too well when I tried out. I got cut but like most people who are cut I thought I was better than a lot of people who made it. I can't honestly say now. At the time I thought I got screwed.

For some reason I could always hit and it was almost impossible to strike me out. My senior year at Prin found me in great shape and finally ready to play. One thing I had learned that Freshman year was how to look like a ballplayer. How to spit, adjust, wiggle and waggle. I played second base. I didn't have a particularly strong arm, but it was accurate. We actually set a school record for double plays, but it was always in doubt that I would get it to first on time. We actually had a good team, but we didn't have a pitcher. Nobody ever lasted too long. No matter how good you are, without a pitcher you won't win and we didn't. It was very frustrating.

The main pitchers were Ty Anderson and Jim Hanlin who took turns playing short stop or third base. One day while practicing at Taylor Field I told coach that I believed I could pitch and to give me a try. He knew how powerful my arm was so he laughingly said that I could pitch batting practice that day. First he wanted to see what kind of stuff I had. He took the catcher's mitt and crouched behind the plate. "Okay Salveter, lets see what you've got", he said. I knew I could get the ball over the plate, but I had never knowingly got a ball to curve, and my fast ball wouldn't scare anyone. However, I had actually learned to throw a "knuckle ball". A knuckle ball is unpredictable in its flight. The strings don't spin. In fact there is an absence of spin or rotation on the ball. I threw him my knuckle ball. It floated in there right over the plate, and then took a severe dip. The ball went under his glove, and hit poor old coach in a very bad spot. He was rolling in agony. I was ready to head for the next county. He got up. Gave me a look and ordered me back to second base.

During a couple of our games we knew that there were pro scouts in the stands. I certainly played a little harder with that knowledge. One day both girls that I had been dating came to a game. It made me very nervous. From my spot at second base I had to look to my left or past first base to see what was going on in the stands. About the time that I looked over there the batter hit a line drive that almost took my head off. I was lucky I didn't get killed, and needless to say coach was not happy.

I was obsessed with not striking out. One day I was called out on a third strike. It was not a strike, and I argued with the umpire. He threw me out of the game and coach ordered me off the field, and into the bus until the game was over. I never felt so frustrated. It's a good thing that the ump and coach couldn't hear what I was saying on that bus. It was a long ride home, and I never argued with the ump again.

Drury didn't have a baseball team, so I didn't play in college. I continued to play pickup games in the summers, and of course good old Indian ball. After I became a lawyer they had tryouts for a "semi-pro team" here in Springfield, and I made it. We played all around. It was harder to play after all the softball I played. That lasted two years, and disbanded. Teddy was just a little guy and sitting in the dugout. I was at bat and heard this terrible screaming. He had gotten up, and while heading for me, the guy on deck hit him in the head with his bat. That really unnerved me.

My baseball career was over except that in May, 1983, we had a baseball reunion at Principia. Coach Schubert was there, and a lot of former players from the years 1950-1956. We played a game that involved the alumni and the current varsity. Carl Osterloh still thought he could pitch, and was on the other team. My first time up all I wanted to do was not look stupid or fall down when I swung. We had a batting practice that morning, and I had been hitting pretty well. I just took a nice level cut at an Osterloh fast ball, and hit it over the centerfield fence about 375' out. It was the only homer hit in that game. The old coach was impressed. Now my baseball career was really over.

1954 Principia Ted 1st Row 3rd from right

TENNIS

Most people who have known me for the last 50 years would easily identify me with tennis, but tennis was not a part of my childhood. As a result of taking it up late in life it has never been completely natural to me. My children grew up playing tennis with a court in their yard. To them it is natural.

There are some first things that one never forgets, but I can't remember the first time I was actually on a tennis court hitting balls. The first time I remember was in the Spring of 1954 right before I graduated from Principia. My friend Ty Anderson, who is a natural athlete, played tennis. I asked him to show me how. I didn't think there would be much to it. The Lodge was the boys dorm, and beside it was a single court. I borrowed one of Ty's rackets and out we went. What I thought would be simple turned out to be impossible. I either couldn't hit the ball at all or when I did I never knew where it would go. Ty thought it was great (me being humbled so), but I was totally embarrassed. The big jock looked like a big jerk. I gave up the game.

When I started Drury in the Fall of 1954 I became good friends with Lanny Benson from Sedalia, who was also there on a basketball scholarship. He didn't know anything about tennis either, but for some reason we decided to start playing. At first we were equally bad, and we would bet on our games. We bet a quart of beer a set. (Students didn't just drink a bottle of beer back then, we drank quarts). For a while nobody was much ahead on the bets, but then I started to get a lot better, and he never won. At one time he owed me 53 quarts of beer and never paid off.

Once in a while I would play with other people. I still didn't know how to play, but I got the ball back and could run down everything. I played for Sig Ep in the inter-fraternity matches. It seems nobody in the house was very good. I won several of those matches, and was champion one year. When my basketball career and track career ended, I really got desperate to get a varsity letter in something, so I decided to give tennis a serious try. My junior year at Drury I went to the public library, and checked out the only book they had on tennis. It was by Don Budge, and even in 1956-57 was very old. They had long pants on in all the illustrations. I bought a "heavy" racket from some guy for $5.00. (Today they try to make them as light as they can. To be macho, I wanted a heavy racket).

Drury had a handball court in the gym. Me, Don Budge and the heavy racket went in there almost every day, and for hours I would hit the ball against the wall the way Don said to do it. I got to where I could swing the heavy racket pretty hard. I was still strong in those days.

When Spring of 1957 rolled around, I was ready to try out for the team. All those people showed up and the coach (Gerald Perry), had everybody playing everybody else until it got down to the top 5 guys. I was number 4. I had made the team. Mick Lloyd was number 5 and was the "alternate". Dick Heimberger was number 1, Larry Pigg was number 2, Ivan Millstead was number 3. Then I started beating Ivan so I became number 3. Rich and Larry played 1 doubles and Ivan and I played 2 doubles. So each time there were 6 matches. I don't remember poor Mick ever getting to play.

There was an open challenge rule at Drury so that anyone in the school could challenge the bottom guy and replace him on the team. We could challenge within the team. I had a left handed fraternity brother named Bob Bridges from Massachusetts. He and I would play occasionally, and once in a while he would beat me. He always wanted to challenge me to get on the team, but he had to challenge Mick. He couldn't challenge me. It made him so mad, because he could never beat Mick, and never got on the team that year.

That year we played the University of Arkansas twice. We were a little outclassed, and never won either match. I was the only one to win a set. The guy I played on their team was also an all Southwest Conference center on the football team. I can't remember his name but he was a good athlete and a nice guy. When we played in Fayetteville it was when they were having Spring football practice. He got out of it because he was on the tennis team. We dressed out with the football team and they were giving him a bad time. When we walked by their practice field to the courts they all good naturedly booed him. We went 3 sets in both matches but he won.

I didn't know my kids would go to William Jewell, heck I didn't even know I would have kids. On May 4, 1957 we played Jewell at Drury. I knew right away that my opponent was a better player than I was, but I also knew that skill didn't always determine who won. When I figured out I couldn't play with him the normal way I decided to use "tactics", also known as "gamesmanship". I started hitting him high lobs on every shot (moon balls). At first he just smacked overhead winners but pretty soon he started missing those. He got very upset with me (I don't blame him), and before long his game and composure were completely gone. I felt bad, but I won.

During a match against Pittsburgh State at Drury I was really into impressing several female students who were watching me play. I was hitting hard and grunting loud. I moved in to kill a forehand, and took a vicious swing from low to high. Unfortunately the racket partially slipped out of my hand, and I hit myself between the eyes with the racket. I can tell you that it hurt like hell, but with the said females watching, I refused to show any pain, although I almost knocked myself out. When I noticed everybody gasping and getting sick, I realized that I was bleeding profusely all over myself.

The match was stopped to bandage me up and clean me up. No stitches though. I was a Marine!

The season ended with the MCAU Conference tournament at Missouri Valley College on May 10 and 11, 1957. By now my game was getting much better and I was routinely beating Heimberger and Pigg. However, I went to the tournament as a very low seed and drew Missouri Valley's No. 1 singles player, some guy from Peru. As if that wasn't bad enough, the courts at Missouri Valley were clay. I had never played on a clay court. Peruvians are clay court specialists, and it was this guy's home court.

Heimberger and Pigg quickly lost their first round matches. Millstead didn't show up so I had no one to play doubles with and had to default. Things were looking pretty bleak, and Dick and Larry were ready to drive back to Drury as soon as I lost. But somehow I won. Nobody could believe it. I ran down everything he hit and just refused to lose. I kept winning, and we stayed over to the next day. I made it to the semi-finals, and played the No. 2 singles player from Westminster. They had a strong team. I gave him a good match, but my luck ran out and he beat me. He won the tournament by beating his team mate the No. 1 singles player. A bad footnote to the end of the season was that the KA's ran the Sou' Wester staff, and so when they took the team pictures they didn't tell me, and stuck Jim Ollis in there. Of course, he didn't play tennis. I'm not sure why I didn't beat the devil out of somebody over that. They didn't tell Mick Lloyd either. Everyone in the golf and tennis team pictures was a KA. I did finally get a Drury Varsity letter so that goal was accomplished.

It was a big deal to be invited to play on Sunday afternoons at Doc Busiek's courts on Walnut Street. I got invited while at Drury, and got beat by some 70 year old man. I was very nervous.

I played tennis a few times in law school, and once in a while after we moved to Springfield and started our family. I was about 33 when I gave up golf, and decided to play serious tennis again. When I was in the Legislature (1968-1971), I would play tennis with some of the guys in Jefferson City. They were Bill Royster of Kansas City, John Schneider and Wayne Goode of St. Louis and Ron Reed from St. Joseph. Occasionally there were others.

It's impossible to recount all the tournaments that I have played in and won. I've had a pretty good run at it, and my office and home are filled with trophies of one sort or another. I'm sure there is a story behind each victory, and even if I could remember them I wouldn't bore the reader with all that. I've bored my wife Sharon with those tales of glory through the years. I don't know what will become of the trophies after I'm gone. When my grandson, Brennon Anthony Salveter was 4 years old, I gave him a trophy and told him to be careful with it. Before he had it too long he broke the racket off it. He told his mother, Lisa, not to worry because "Paw Paw will give me another One". He was right, but I told him no more. Any others he would have to earn himself.

I played a lot of sports without any serious injury, but tennis has taken its toll. In 1989 I tore the cartilage in my left knee and had it operated on. Then, shortly after Tony was killed, I tore the cartilage in my right knee and had it operated on. The knee injuries stopped me from jogging or running, but I didn't stop playing tournament tennis. In 1993 I made a comeback, and had a great year. I ended up being ranked No. 3 in 55 singles in the Missouri Valley. This includes, Missouri, Oklahoma, Nebraska, Kansas and Iowa. But the knees were too bad to keep that up, and I didn't play tournaments in 1994.

In 1995 I decided to try again and started out by winning 4 of the first 5 tournaments I played in. The pain was too great, and I quit again by July 1995. It was strange to be playing so well, but having to quit. I finally ended up just playing doubles a couple of times a week, and finally gave it up for good in 2002. Some of the younger guys I played with when I quit were Jim Penn, Fred Dupy, Kevin Burrington, John Clouse, Jeff Gunderson, Jack Bagby, Mike Punzell, Don Creek, Randy Allen, Tim Callaway, Phil Pierce, Joe Larson and Harry Phelps.

A lot of guys that I played with for years are gone now. I have fond memories of Gerald Perry, Clay Anderson, Strat Harrison,

"Doc" Busiek, Erwin and Paul Busiek, Walt Watkins, Earl Nau, Ken Soxman Mike Green and Salty Pinnell. Some that are still around that I don't see much are Gene Paine, Sam Cox, Charles Kimbro, Jack Harrison, Richard Fronabarger, Rich and Randy Bachus, Glen Rippee, Steve Grace, Doug Fuller, C. B. Raynes, Bob Powers, Jerry Lowther, Tom Hornbuckle, Major Close, Craig Oliver, Jerry Morgan, Bob Burlingame, Gerry Perry and others.

A lot of fun and serious tennis was played on our court at 1635 E. Delmar. The kids all became good players on that court, and we had many a good set of "family doubles". Tom Essman, Bob Thurman, Tung Nguyen, and a lot of other kids played there. Sharon and her students and friends played too. There are a lot of happy memories of the old court and pool.

GOLF

I lay no claim to being a good golfer, but like most duffers I will occasionally play a hole like it was meant to be played. This always gives me hope that my game is finally on the verge of a great turnaround. It never is. My excuse used to be that if I had more time, and could play a lot and practice, I would be good. That didn't help much.

My Dad played some golf, and my first exposure to the game was as his caddie or just following him around the course. He used to play at Forest Park in St. Louis or Waterloo Country Club in Illinois. Eventually I started playing there too. I never had any lessons, and just picked up pointers along the way. I put together a set of old castaway clubs (some wooden) and did my best. I probably was around 12 years old when I started playing.

We used to sneak on to Kendrick Seminary's course and play until the priests kicked us off. Dave Schuette lived on Swon near there, so Dave and I played and so did Dick Bell and others. That was just a nine hole course with sand greens. A lot of courses in those days had sand greens. Waterloo did. It was cheaper than grass. You had to rake a smooth path to the hole before you could putt. The sand was supposed to be wet so it would hold approach shots well. This probably explains why so many of my balls end up in sand traps now.

When I came to Drury, I would occasionally play at Grandview with Ron Ollis and others. We used to play at different courses in St. Louis such as University City. Once in high school Oscar Sample asked me to play at Greenbrier Country Club in Kirkwood. His folks were members. He had a brand new set of clubs, and there I was with my crummy set. He got real mad after hitting about 5 balls in a row into a water hazard, and proceeded to smash each one of his clubs into a tree and throw them into the water. I would have been thrilled to have those clubs.

I played some in law school, usually with Joe Teasdale. We were pretty even, and have played at some of our law school reunions with, Joe, Hank Luepke, John McCartney, Paul Simon and others.

The most serious golf I played was after I started practicing law in Springfield. I was 24 and several young lawyers played every weekend at Grandview or Siler's. That group consisted of John Lewis, Hank Westbrooke, John Crow, Bob Schroff, Willis Graven and Jack Yocum. We had a lot of fun, and our quarter bets got pretty contested with lots of heckling and huckles. One day at Grandview I gave Willis Graven a dime to spot his ball with on the green, and to this day I have not been able to get it back. Success killed our group because one by one the guys decided they should be playing with potential clients and not other lawyers. So we started joining country clubs. I joined Twin Oaks.

At Twin Oaks I got too serious about golf. I probably played 4 times a week. Sharon played too, and the boys played some. I had a regular group at Twin Oaks, and of course there was gambling going on. The amounts were higher so the pressure to win was greater. Fortunately there were a few guys in my group who had more money than sense and ability and I usually won. I played a lot with Gary Fredrick, Wilson Allison, Bob Smith, Bob Schroff, Jim Prewitt, Neil Stenger and a lot of others.

One day after playing 18 holes and a few card games I was in the shower - locker room, and noticed that male golfers seemed to have little pot bellies, thin legs, and spindly asses. I was 33, and didn't want to end up this way, so I quit - totally, and started playing a lot of tennis instead. It was about 30 years before I played golf again. In the Fall of 1995 I was playing in an Evangel College tournament at Horton Smith, and won my first golf trophy for 1st place in "C" flight. What can I say? When I retired in 1997 I started playing a lot with Bob Kinloch, Jack VanHook and Cecil Mooney. They were merciless and have a lot of my money. In 2000 we rejoined Twin Oaks, and I play a lot now. In that same year I also joined the Springfield Senior Golf Association, and have enjoyed that as well. Golf is the only competitive out let that I have now. Tackling is not allowed. I have two holes in one. One at No. 15 at Twin Oaks, and one at No. 4 at Stewart.

1998 Pines Golf Course, Virginia. Ted Salveter and John Lewis.

1999 Twin Oaks Country Club. Bob Kinloch, Jack VanHook, Ted Salveter, Tom Wyrick

SOFTBALL

Did this guy do anything but play you might wonder? Of course we played softball on the playgrounds of grade school. I remember games at Lockwood. I especially remember the annual "Play Day" when 5th and 6th grades were broken up into teams and numerous games, and competitions were played for a whole day. One team would come out on top. Softball was part of it, and I remember hitting a home run over the center field fence. Those were the days.

In junior high and high school we played softball as part of our Physical Ed classes. No gloves - played bare handed with an oversize ball. The fraternity had a softball team and we weren't bad. I remember that my sophomore or junior year we challenged the Sig Eps at SMS to a game with a keg of beer as the prize. We colonized that chapter which was primarily made up of the SMS football team. It was a good game until a tackle named Kazmarak tagged up at third and tried to score on a sacrifice fly. The throw to me at the plate was high, and he could have easily scored without hitting me. Instead he hit me in the air going full speed, and knocked me on the fly into the backstop. That pretty much ended the game for me.

I played on our Webster Baptist Church team in law school, and when we moved to Springfield in 1960 I played a lot of softball. University Heights Baptist had a good team. Larry Perkins was our pitcher and I caught. He really messed up my fingers with his drop and rise balls. Every body recruited players on those church teams, and after a while it got to be a joke. The games were not played with a "Christian" atmosphere. There were lots of fights, and lots of swearing. The level of softball was pretty good.

After I took the bar exam in Jefferson City at the end of June 1960, I came straight to Springfield and started work the next day. I got on a team that had no sponsor in an independent league. We were a really good team and won our league. Back then they had a playoff system to determine the City Champion. We made it to the finals, and played the News-leader AAA team, and only got beat 3-2.

I played on a lot of different teams, and usually played second base. I had been spiked in the hand on a play at second base, and after that I couldn't play for a while. When I came back I had trouble gripping the bat. We were in the playoffs again against a AAA team, and with my bad hand I hit the winning home run over the centerfield fence. I was always a good hitter in baseball and softball.

After many years of enjoying fast pitch softball, a thing called "slow-pitch" softball came along. It became so popular that virtually no one played fast pitch anymore. For a purest like me that was too much. I tried it for a while, but there was just no challenge. The thing about slow pitch is you don't have to be able to hit, and you don't need a real pitcher or catcher. A lot of big guys with beer bellies now play because even they can hit a ball that is lobbed up to them. There are a lot of home runs because the teams are made up of big guys with beer bellies. I decided that this was not softball and quit. This was okay because it was interfering with my tennis anyway.

HANDBALL, RACQUETBALL, ETC.

I never heard of handball before I started Drury, but there was one court there and I learned to play. In law school I played at SLU with Joe Teasdale, John McCartney and Gus Luepke. After I came to Springfield I joined the YMCA and played there. I played in a lot of tournaments and won a few trophies. I got to be a high B player and almost an A player. Some of the guys I played a lot with were Hans Taylor, Jack Webster, Saul Nuccitelli, Kerry Montgomery, Larry Giboney, Earl Nau, Barry Aton, Phil Wannemacher and a lot of others. It was very popular. Then along came racquetball, and handball sort of died out. My favorite handball story is back when my friend Joe Teasdale was Governor. When he'd come to town we'd get together and jog or play handball.

Joe was always guarded wherever he went by a highway patrol trooper. One time Joe had a guy with him from Kansas City (Aylward) who was in a powerful family, and was a big contributor. The three of us played "cutthroat" while the trooper watched from above. This guy was a real jerk (at least that day), and was doing all kinds of illegal stuff during the game. He was a big guy like Joe. I was getting steamed, but because of Joe I was trying to ignore it. Then the guy literally knocked me over going for a ball. I came up swinging, and Joe was trying to break it up. The trooper was panicked because he couldn't get to the governor from up there, and the whole thing got out of hand.

I switched to racquetball too. It was a natural for me, because it is a cross between handball and tennis. I did okay and even won a few tournaments, but I never really got excited about it, and eventually I quit that too.

SKIING

I learned to water ski in the 7th grade at Lake Norfolk at the Blue Waters Resort at Henderson, Arkansas. I used to do a lot of it in college, and the early years after I started practicing law. I quit after my knee surgeries.

I was pretty old (37) the first time I went snow skiing. A bunch of us piled into Walt Forester's Motor Home, and drove to Breckenridge, Colorado. We all took our kids. I believe it was Walt Forester, Curtis Graff and me and maybe Bill Mullis. I took Teddy, Tony and Paige. They had never skied. This was probably in 1973. Paige was 6, Teddy was 12 and Tony 9 or 10.

We all took lessons in ski school, but Tony got altitude sickness, and threw up in the snow. He had to sit out and didn't get to ski again until the last day. We had a good time, and the kids kept going back every year. I did too but not as often. When my knees got bad, I almost gave it up. The last time was in 1994. I am an okay skier, but very cautious. Paige thinks that I only know how to snow plow. I am always thankful when I finish a run that I hadn't broken anything. I have skied at Breckenridge, Vail, Winter Park, Copper Mountain, Keystone and Wolf Creek. The last time was after Christmas in 1994 when Sharon and I took Teddy, Lisa, Rachael, Brennon, Paige and Dan to Wolf Creek, Colorado. We had a great time. Sharon tried to ski again, but couldn't do it. Neither could Lisa. Brennon was too young, and Rachael loved it. We stayed at Fairfield in Pagossa Springs.

Skiing is very exhilarating, but it can be dangerous. I have always enjoyed it, but I can live without it. Paige believes it is her God given right to ski at least twice every year. So did Tony.

Ted and granddaughter Rachael Salveter at Wolf Creek Pass Colorado, 1994.

I believe that sports and games have added a lot to my life, and have made life more fun and interesting. Even ping pong, badminton and pool get the blood pumping. It all keeps you healthy and alert. I will keep at it as long as I can. There's hardly a sport I haven't played. I never played Lacrosse, squash, cricket or polo. Maybe it's time.

1955 Drury Track Team

Ted 1st row 3rd from right

CHAPTER THREE

•Farm Life•

My beginnings were pretty humble. I was born May 5, 1936 at St. Francis Hospital in Washington, Missouri. I was a Great Depression baby. Times were hard. Washington was the town in which my mother, Nelda Marie Anna Oberhaus grew up. Old Doc Mays brought me into this world. I suppose that means there was a young Doc Mays. I don't know. He also delivered my brother Charles Robert 5 years later. Mom and Dad had been married a couple of years before they had me. She was 18 and he 25. I was named Theodore Clifton Salveter, III after my grandfather. I named my first born "IV", but when he had a son June 14, 1991, he broke the tradition and instead of "V" it was Brennon Anthony Salveter. I don't know where the Brennon came from but "Anthony" was for my second son, Philip Anthony Salveter, who died March 8, 1990. My Dad never could understand that, and asked me about it until he died on July 8, 1995.

Until I was married most people called me "Skip". My mom would call me "Skipper" when I was in trouble. This was a nick name my aunt Helen Wardan supposedly gave to me. I was never called Skip at Principia however. I guess it wasn't dignified enough. If someone calls me Skip today I know that it is someone who has known me for a long time.

We didn't live in Washington. My grandfather Salveter owned a farm at Gray Summit Missouri, and we lived there. Grandpa wasn't a farmer mind you, although he liked to ride the mules, no he was a traveling salesman. Imagine, a traveling salesman who had his own farm! There's a joke there somewhere. My grandmother was May B. (Bradley) Salveter, and we lived on the farm with them. This closeness enabled them to spoil me rotten, and I remained close to them until they died.

We lived on the farm until I was about 6 years old and ready to start the first grade. I didn't go to kindergarten because they didn't have one at Gray Summit. My Dad was the farmer. He truly loved it. Mom probably wasn't so crazy about it. He had cattle and hogs and raised some crops. We had a black family, Jess's family, that lived on the place, and worked for Dad. They had kids who were pretty much my only playmates. I don't know what the arrangement was between Dad and grandpa, but when grandpa wouldn't sell the farm to him, and instead sold it to someone else, the feelings weren't too good, and Dad was no longer a farmer. He never farmed again, but that was always his dream. In some ways he was consumed by it. He knew all about farming until the day he died. I don't know how he knew.

I am sure that what I remember about the farm is influenced by stories I have heard others tell, and yet there are lots of things I do remember. I wandered off once with my 2 dogs "Fat Puppy" and "Freckles". I remember being out there in those woods not having a clue where I was or how to get home. The folks were pretty frantic, and a search party was looking for me. I was found. That's how come I'm here now. My parents acted very strange. They were crying and very glad they found me, but once they got all the hugs and kisses out of the way they spanked the tar out of me for wandering off. It took some of the luster off being found.

There were lots of dogs and animals around the farm. We had a big German Sheppard named "Fritz". He loved me, and was very protective. He saved my life. Honest. Here's what happened. We had an old model A or T or some kind of car parked in the driveway. Dad got in it to back out and go somewhere, and I crawled over behind the car. He couldn't see me, but before he backed over me, Fritz acted like Lassie, grabbed my clothes with his teeth, and pulled me out of the way. When Dad realized what he had almost done, he was sick. Fritz was a hero and Dad was always more careful before he moved the car or anything else.

Well almost. There was the hog house incident. He had these A frame hog house's which he could move around by attaching a team of mules or a tractor to them by chain. Well he set about to drag one off, (they had no floor) but didn't check inside. Guess who was playing inside? Yeah, me. When he pulled it I screamed bloody murder because it got pulled over me. He almost got me again, but he leaped off that tractor, and even though that hog house was too heavy for him to lift, he did it anyway. Amazing what you can do when you are 240 lbs., and scared to death. Outside of being pretty shook up, I guess I wasn't hurt too bad. Grandpa and grandma were pretty upset with him though. And they should have been.

We had two mules that did a lot of work around the farm, but you could saddle them, and ride them too. Grandpa loved to ride. He was pretty much a gentlemen farmer. We had a big "mounting block" in the front yard out by the road. This was used by little people and girls to mount the mule or horse from. Sometimes he'd put 3 or 4 of us on that mule. The mules pulled farm equipment and a big wagon Dad had. He'd even harness that baby up and take it into town to Gray Summit, or Labadie to get supplies and stuff. Just like in the movies.

One time Dad took me in the wagon to the General Store in Labadie. Even though we had Jess and his family on the place, Dad would let a comment slip about blacks now and then. There was this big black man in the store, and like a little parrot I repeated some of Dad's stuff. This pretty well steamed this guy at me (I was 4 or 5), and at Dad. He had to be restrained, and Dad and I got the heck out of there. Be careful what you say and do around your kids.

The old farm house is still there and occupied. It sort of sticks out like a sore thumb because it is surrounded by a subdivision. The mounting block is there too. It all looked a lot better when it was surrounded by nothing but farmland 70 years ago. Across the road from our farm was the Purina Mills Experimental Farms. Ralston Purina had a big farm where they field tested everything from chicken feed to dog food. We used to go over there. One thing I remember were multicolored little chicks and bunny rabbits. They were probably an Easter specialty. A friend of the family, Emmit Pursley, worked there. His wife's name was Onita. They lived in St. Clair. Purina also raised chinchillas, minks, fox and other animals women make coats out of.

There was a Holecamp Lumber Company in Gray Summit, and Bob and Vera Holecamp were friends of my parents. They had Bobby and Marty who were older than me. Bobby was killed in St. Louis when he fell off a truck in front of a street car. Marty became like a sister to me, and years later both families lived in Webster Groves.

I remember going with Dad to gather eggs from the hen house and finding a big black snake trying to swallow an egg whole. Apparently his mother never taught him to cut up his food and take smaller bites. Mom was always trying to kill snakes with a rake or a hoe. She was usually pretty excited when swinging that rake. Seems like there were a lot of snakes around there. I remember eating lunch one day, and stepping out the back door right on one sunning himself on the back step. That got me and the snake moving pretty fast.

I don't guess that we had all the modern conveniences. We must have had indoor plumbing because I don't remember an outhouse, and to this day I couldn't picture my opera singing petite grandma Salveter using one. Water had to be heated on the stove, and baths were taken in a big wash tub in the kitchen. The place was heated by a wood stove in the living room and a cook stove in the kitchen. The bedrooms were cold. We got our water from a cistern out back. I'm not sure how all that worked.

We went into Washington and stayed with my mom's parents Henry and Christina Oberhaus a lot. Grandpa Oberhaus was not a big man, and as long as I knew him he was always badly stooped over. This may be why my mother was always telling me to "stand up straight". Grandpa obviously had poor posture. Who knows, he may have been 6'5"! Grandma Oberhaus was a big German woman, and from my perspective seemed to run things. Grandpa owned an orange brick building on the corner of Hooker and the main highway that ran through the town. It was 2 stories, and they lived on the second floor. It looked a lot like the place in "Lost In Yonkers". On the first floor was grandpa's shoe shop, and a small neighborhood grocery store. I remember running all around the place.

Grandpa and Grandma Oberhaus were very kind and gentle people. They were generous to a fault. Especially grandma. Dad always wondered why Henry put up with it. Of course, Dad was one of those people she was always feeding. She was a great cook, and one thing she made that I really liked was rice and tomato soup. She was always hovering over the table making sure everyone kept eating. She would always say "Just eat"! We all did. Grandpa was always loaning money to people. A lot of them never paid him back. They had favorite places they liked to take me. At the "Blue Goose" I'd get orange soda, cheese and crackers. We'd also go to Lottmans where the specialty was big roast beef sandwiches. On Saturday night they would take me while they played pinochle. There was a corn cob pipe factory in Washington, and we'd get stuff from there once in a while too. Grandpa always smoked cigars. Today I couldn't stand that, but back then a lot of the men smoked, and it was more accepted.

There is a big city park in Washington down near the Missouri River, and the railroad tracks. We used to go over there for fish fries and carnivals and stuff. There is a swimming pool there, and I unofficially learned how to swim in that pool. They moved to a house near that park, and that is the house where grandma died when I was about 12. Washington is a river town and a railroad town. It really was when I was a young boy. The trains and boats were always a great fascination for me. Years later we used to take the train from St. Louis to Washington. I always liked to help grandpa in his shoe shop. The smell of the leather and glue, and the noise of the sewing machine were unforgettable.

The Tobins were Grandma Oberhaus' side of the family, and there were a lot of Tobins and Oberhaus around Washington in those days. I remember that her brother, Uncle Frank Tobin, had a shop behind his house, and he supported the family by making brooms. Times certainly seemed simpler back then.

One time Grandpa Salveter took me to the General Store at Labadie. They took it upon themselves to make sure that I always minded my manners, knew proper etiquette and spoke "distinctly". As we left the store grandpa reminded me to say goodbye. I didn't do it. He reminded me again. Nothing. He really reminded me, and when that failed he kicked me square in the rear at which point I wheeled around and shouted "Goodbye"! I wasn't always perfect.

Life on the farm those first 6 years of my life, during the Depression, left a strong imprint on me even though it is a long ago dim memory. I've never really had a desire to be a farmer, but I have a love of the country, and small town life that probably borders on the nostalgic.

I could be quite content on a farm doing the hard labor required. I don't mind the work, and I don't mind the smells. But when I wanted to get away I would want to be free to leave. A real farmer is shackled to it, and I would not like that.

1939. Grandfather with Skip and friends. Mule and mounting block.

1940. Skip and hog house.

CHAPTER FOUR

•My Old Kentucky Home•

When the farm thing didn't work out for Dad, he got a job as a salesman for Ralston Purina. Yes, he worked for the original old man Danforth. The job caused us to move to Mayfield, Kentucky when I was about 6 years old. This would have been in 1942. I started school in Mayfield. First grade. I went to two grade schools in Mayfield because we moved across town. One of them was Washington Park School. I can't remember the other. I had a history of fighting in school, and it all started on the very first day.

I didn't know any of the kids, being new in town, and this little rich kid sat in front of me. We were pretty poor, and he kept turning around and showing me his new valise, crayons, paper, etc., and asking why I didn't have anything. It was getting embarrassing, and annoying. Finally when I could take it no longer I slugged him and we knocked over several desks. It was not a good start.

I don't remember much about the school except that the PTA

had a baby contest, and my little brother Charles won 1st prize as the cutest baby. He got a blue ribbon for that. I was only a little jealous. I remember that even though we were Christian Scientists they made me get a vaccination before I could start school. It was the old kind on your arm that got all infected and had a big scab. For a kid who never went to a doctor this was a big deal. I remember my first Halloween at school. We all wore our costumes to school. Mom made me an orange and black clown outfit.

Switching schools after my first year was very hard on me and I remember being very scared that first day at the other school. My stomach was more than a little queasy as Mom led me into this strange place. This was in the South, and they eat a lot of weird things there, like turnip greens. There is nothing worse. As we walked into the school, the cooks were already preparing lunch. The smell of the cooking turnip greens started to make me sick. Even as I am writing this the thought makes me sick. Before Mom could get me to the principal's office I started throwing up. Again, my first day at school was off to a bad start.

Judge Duckworth's son or grandson was a friend of mine. He and I played a lot together. There were a bunch of older boys that we would spy on. They had a club and cooked stuff. We saw where they hid their matches, and decided we could cook potatoes. We set this field on fire. The high grass started to burn, and we tried desperately to stomp it out. We couldn't, and the fire circle grew very fast. Finally, we gave up and ran as fast as we could to my house where we sat on the couch in the living room, very much out of breath. Mom asked what we were doing. "Sitting". The fire truck went by with siren blaring and lights flashing. We must have looked guilty because she asked what we knew about it, and we said, "nothin".

It wasn't long before we were answering questions from the police and fire department. You see, we had been spotted running from the fire. Mr. Hodges' garage burned down, but they saved his house. It's a good thing we knew a judge.

The Guy Koonce family were good friends of my parents. He had an insurance agency. The Roberts lived next door to us at our second house. They owned a funeral home, and were particularly fond of my little brother Charles. It was at this house that he made his famous statement, "There's a spider on the corncrink". Some store across the street had a big parrot that sat out front on a perch all day. I never trusted that bird, and I didn't like what it had to say.

We used to go to Kentucky Lake for picnics. Sometimes we'd go to Padukah. Dad would always tell me "that's the home of Albin Barkley". In case you forgot, Albin Barkley was Harry Truman's Vice President. I think that life in Mayfield must have been very normal, but I don't remember much. It was the county seat and always busy. One Saturday Dad ran over a little boy on the square. He wasn't killed, but was hurt badly. It was the kid's fault, but Dad never got over it. It was 1943 or 1944 when we left Mayfield and moved to St. Louis, Missouri.

Skip, Charles and Mom, Mayfield Kentucky, 1943.

CHAPTER FIVE

•St. Louis•

We moved into a flat on Big Bend in Richmond Heights near Clayton Road. It was a pretty rough neighborhood. I went to Belleview School for part of the 2nd and 3rd grade. I believe that I got in a fight almost every day there, either at school or coming and going. It was like a war zone. The second World War was still going on, and Dad had a job as an inspector at McDonald Douglas. He was not drafted because he was a little too old, and because he had bad feet and allergies. The fights were so bad that I remember finally getting a pipe away from a kid who had me on the ground trying to hit me with it, when his father intervened, and gave him the pipe back.

Lots of really bad stuff happened to me in that neighborhood. One time this guy got me in his house (I'm 2nd grade right?), and started chasing me with a big butcher knife. Somehow I got out of there. At 7 or 8 years old I had to go to the police station, and identify him in a police line up. The scuddiest people in the world were the Hueys who lived in a house behind our flat. Who knows how many kids they had. They would think nothing of walking onto their back porch in the nude or urinating and defecating in their back yard. Dad always made jokes about the Hueys. But one day a bunch of their kids talked me into going into their house. The place was a pig sty with human waste all over the floor. I don't know how anyone could live in those conditions. I wanted out of there, but they wouldn't let me go. They made me stay in that house for hours. I was traumatized. I don't know why they decided to finally let me go, but they did. The police did nothing.

My brother Charles used to play with the little girl who lived on the first floor of our flat. She seemed so cute and innocent. Little Rusty Lewis. One day she buried a hatchet in his forehead between the eyes, and almost killed him.

My dentist's office was a few blocks west of our flat on Big Bend. I hated to go to the dentist. I went there by myself. Can you imagine? I got real nervous sitting in his waiting room. When he got me in the chair, he told me he had to pull one of my teeth. He yanked around, but it didn't come out. I was in a panic, and I jumped out of the chair, ran screaming through his waiting room full of patients, and ran all the way home. I'm sure that little scene was not good for his business. The tooth still hurt so Mom made another appointment. This time she took me and made sure I stayed. After he pulled it I thought I was going to bleed to death. I had cotton in my mouth for a long time.

The folks had made friends with the Flockins while we were in Mayfield. He was in the army or something and they had been transferred to New Orleans. Mom and I got on a train and traveled to New Orleans to see them. The war was still on and the train was full of soldiers and sailors. I guess Mom would have only been in her late twenties or early thirties. These guys seemed to be paying too much attention to her, so I finally told them that my Mom was married, my Dad was real big, and I had a little brother at home. After that they seemed a lot less interested.

I've never been back to New Orleans since that trip. I remember two things. We went to the Gulf of Mexico, at the seaport there. The ocean was full of Navy ships of all kinds and sizes. There was a battleship, an aircraft carrier, a destroyer, lots of destroyers, PT Boats, and troop ships. For an impressionable young boy it was a fantastic sight. I felt so proud of my country, and so much safer seeing all that raw power. We were all afraid of the Germans and Japanese, so it was good to see all those soldiers, sailors, ships and planes.

The other thing I remember is that old French Quarter with all its history and old buildings. Also an amusement park, where I was scared out of my wits by a huge head of a clown that opened his large mouth, and laughed this sinister laugh. I had nightmares about that clown, and to this day I do not trust clowns. To me they are not funny. However, I do like to "clown around".

On the east side of our flat was a small street or alley. Across the alley was the back of a bowling alley that faced on Clayton Road. It was probably near or next to the Empire Theater. You could hear those bowling balls all night long it seemed. Sometimes I would sneak over there, and the pin boys would open the back door and let me watch. These days there are automatic pin setters, but back then they hired kids to set the pins. It could get dangerous because you might get hit by the ball, or a flying pin, especially if you didn't get out of the way quick enough.

CHAPTER SIX

• Depression And World War II •

W orld War II started long before December 7, 1941, but on that day the Japanese pulled a sneak attack, and attacked our troops and ships at Pearl Harbor. I was 5 years old. The United States was now at war with Japan, and the Germans quickly declared war on us too. The Germans surrendered on May 7, 1945, just two days after my 9th birthday. The Japanese surrendered aboard the battleship Missouri on September 2, 1945. The war was over. We had won.

When the war started, we lived on the farm at Gray Summit. When I was born in 1936 the "Great Depression" was in full bloom. Most people consider it to have started with the stock market crash of 1929, and it was ended by the U.S. entering World War II. The production of war implements, and the employment of our armed forces spurred the economy, and this continued after the war in a long post war boom period.

As a young boy growing up during the Depression and World War II, I developed a lot of fears and opinions. We were poor and there was always this feeling of economic insecurity. Because of the war propaganda I learned to hate the Japanese and Germans. You couldn't trust anybody because they might be spies. At one point in my life I even began to believe that my parents were German spies. That bit of paranoia developed into a belief that they weren't really my parents, just look alikes, that the Germans had planted in our house. I used to check the walls for sounds of secret radios and spy stuff. Yes, you could say that I had a rather active imagination. It didn't help matters that all my relatives on my mother's side were Germans. I was sure that at any moment the Gestapo would come for me and my brother Charles, and no one would hear from us again.

There was this great little song we would sing to the tune of "Whistle While You Work" from Snow White. It went like this:

"Whistle while you work

Hitler is a jerk

Mussolini is a weenie

Tojo is a squirt!"

In school we were urged to save our pennies and dimes to buy government bonds to help pay for the war. We were urged to plant "Victory Gardens" to save food for the boys overseas. We had "rationing". You could only buy limited amounts of sugar, meat, tires, etc. All the stuff that the soldiers needed more than we did. The government would give you stamps, and you had to give up a stamp for each purchase of a rationed item. People used to sell them, trade them and counterfeit them. Lots of stuff was sold on the "black-market". But all in all we loved our country, and most people pitched in to do their part. From this I developed a sense of community, country, and responsibility to my fellow man.

Of course, you can read all about the Depression and War in your history books, but for me it made a great impression. The fear that we might lose to our hated and evil enemies was pretty scary. We cheered as each victory was announced, and when the war was finally over, we felt great relief. We were safe and our boys would be coming home. I had 3 uncles in the war, and all made it okay. Sharon had an uncle, Bob Downen, who was killed in 1943 during the Battle of the Bulge. He was 23. War is a terrible thing. I'm not sure how much we have learned. Individuals and nations still seem to resort to force, violence, bloodshed and war to get their way, and to settle disputes. Sometimes it seems as though the world has gone mad.

CHAPTER SEVEN

•Webster Groves•

We finally got out of that terrible neighborhood in Richmond Heights, and moved in with my uncle and aunt, Charles and Helen Wardan in Webster Groves. They lived at 37 Greeley. It was a wonderful old English Tudor House with a great big yard. I always loved that house. I think it burned down in the 1960s. Even though the house was big, it was pretty crowded when the 4 of us moved in. People did a lot of living with their relatives in those days. My uncle Raymond and aunt Vanetta Oberhaus lived with us in the flat on Big Bend, and later in the house on Summit.

I went to Avery School on the corner of Bompart and Marshall in the 3rd grade. I had measles at that house, and I believe that my cousin Pat Wardan was born while we lived there. Dad was still working at McDonnell-Douglas. I liked Avery School a whole lot better than Belleview School. Webster was so nice compared to the "flat" neighborhood, that it felt like being in Heaven. We couldn't stay there forever, and even though Dad and aunt Helen were brother and sister, I think that they were getting on each others nerves. Eventually Dad bought an old white stucco house at 548 Summit Avenue. It was not the house Mom wanted him to buy, but Dad always intended to get the cheapest thing he could. The other house may have been better, but I thank my lucky stars that we bought a house in Webster Groves, and as it turns out, that little 2 bedroom house is still my favorite place in all the world. My fondest memories are of those days and our life at "548".

We moved into 548 in 1944. The house had been built in 1880 or before. The construction was very poor. Sometimes "they don't build them like they used to" doesn't mean better. I think Dad bought the house from old man Moran who was somewhat of a recluse or invalid. The house looked okay from the outside. It was white stucco, with a screened in porch across the front, and halfway down the north side. That porch was wonderful, and in good weather made the small house seem much bigger. There were two bedrooms, and a bath upstairs. The larger front bedroom was for Mom and Dad. The smaller back bedroom was for Charles and me. The living room was across the front of the house with a dining room and kitchen behind the living room. There was a "butler's pantry" off the rear of the dining room and kitchen. You would have to go through it to get between those two rooms. Although it was a little house, I always thought it was better than it was because it had that Butler's Pantry. It made you feel rich and special imagining that butlers used to wait on prior families of the house just like in the movies. The truth is it was just a glorified broom closet or pantry. The house had a full unfinished basement that seemed to be fully occupied by a huge coal fired furnace. The yard was 75' x 125', and was more than adequate for two boys. There was no garage, but there was a concrete slab in back supporting a chicken house or tool shed. It was about 6' x 15'. There were big trees in the yard, including a pear tree, a wild cherry tree, and a sweet cherry tree. They all gave us a lot of fruit.

The house needed a lot of work, and over the years Dad did the "remodeling" with me as his slave-assistant. Their bedroom floor shook so much when you walked on it that we were always afraid it would fall into the living room. It had an ominous bow or sway to it. Dad didn't want to hire a professional to fix this so he and I took up the floor and nailed in a lot of cross pieces to the floor joists. This stopped the shaking and vibration pretty well, but the floor was as swaybacked as ever.

The house was a story and a half so the roof line was prominent in the bedrooms. Dad and I built a closet along the entire south wall of their bedroom, with two large sliding doors that we also made. The thing actually worked. Then we knocked the old plaster off the walls and put up plasterboard. The floor was "lovely" so we covered it with new linoleum Dad bought in a store in Maplewood. I'm not sure that linoleum was ever a fad in bedrooms, but we apparently didn't know any better. In fact, all the rooms in the house ended up with linoleum, except the living room and dining room which had nice hardwood floors.

The house was hard to heat. That may have been because it was so old it didn't have any insulation. There was an attic which you could get to by crawling through an opening in the ceiling of the upstairs hall. Dad was too big to fit through that so the attic was my job. Of course, now we know that asbestos can cause lung cancer and other diseases. He had me up there pushing insulation that came in bags down the roof and side walls, and then over the entire floor of the attic. I had to nail down some boards to make a floor up there. One time I missed a board when I took a step and my foot came through our bedroom ceiling. That was a horrible, nasty job, but I guess the house was warmer. I used to imagine all kinds of things going on in that attic as I laid in my bed at night. I was pretty sure that's where the Germans had their spy office.

We knocked out a wall in our bedroom to enlarge it, and put up new wallboard. Our beds would fit right under the roof. New wallboard was put up in the kitchen, dining room and living room. A door was knocked in the wall between the dining room and kitchen and the butlers pantry was sealed off from the dining room side.

Through the years things were done to the house. Mom finally had that old bedroom floor replaced, braced and leveled. The folks added a "stoker" to the coal furnace, and finally Mom had it all taken out and a new oil furnace installed. This gave us a lot more room in the basement, and got rid of all that dirty coal. It also eliminated my job of having to take the red hot "clinkers" out of the furnace each day and pound them into little pieces in the back yard out by the back fence where the clothesline was. The oil furnace fed itself so I didn't have to shovel coal into the furnace or the stoker anymore. My life was getting better.

As I grew older, and became an adult with a family and house of my own in Springfield, I would still always think of ways that I would remodel and fix the old house up. I always knew that someday I would move back to Webster and live in 548. When Mom died in 1983 of cancer at the age of 67, Charles and I decided to sell the house. It was one of the hardest things I ever had to do. Many times I wish we hadn't done it. The people who bought it, and those that followed, have screwed it up so badly that I hate to go by and see it when I am in Webster. Maybe I'll buy it back and restore it some day. Maybe not. Anyway it gave us 40 years of wonderful memories. That must be worth something.

I can't assume that the reader knows anything about Webster Groves. It was and still is a unique place. Everyone probably thinks their "hometown" is special, and to them it is. But Webster, even by the account of outsiders, has truly been special. In fact, residents of Webster have always thought so to the irritation of others in the St. Louis area. It has had a reputation of being a place that was "snooty", and where the inhabitants thought that they and their town were better than everyone else. Guilty! We do feel it's the best place in the world to live. To illustrate what I mean, there was this song that students sang at various pep rallies etc. I'm not sure about the spelling.

"Aiyi kiyikus, nobody like us, we are the team from

Webster Hi. Always a winning, always a grinning,

   always a feeling fine. Ki Yi!!!"

The population of this St. Louis suburb has changed through the years. It was probably between 25,000 and 30,000 people when I was growing up there. Over the years the population aged, in that there were more adults and older people than children and young adults. It is a fairly expensive place to live, with property values being higher than surrounding areas. It is primarily a residential community with people working somewhere else. There is no industry, but a lot of shops and small local businesses. There are four distinct areas in the town that at one time were little communities of their own. They are the Marshall Avenue area, Old Orchard, downtown Webster and Little Webster on Big Bend. We lived between the Marshall and Old

Orchard area.

The whole St. Louis area was part of the Louisiana Purchase in 1803. Settlement of the Webster area started in the 1840's. Although a recognizable community, and a cluster of communities, it wasn't until 1896 that the town was officially chartered. It is a community that has always been proud of its schools, and boasts one of the finest public school systems in the State of Missouri. It also has Webster University and Eden Seminary in addition to several private schools including Narrinx Hall a Catholic girl's school. Its Loretto-Hilton Theater is nationally known, and it has an active community theater. In 1965 CBS thought it such a different place that it produced a program called "16 In Webster Groves" that aired nationally. In the 70's David Hartman stared as "Lucas Tanner", a TV show based on the life of a Webster Groves high school teacher. For me to grow up in a place like this during a special time in the nation's history, the 1940's and 50's, was a blessing and a privilege. No one can turn back the clock, but as I look back on my life, and see how it was shaped by this unique time and place, I feel good and lucky to have so lived.

The Salveters were a definite part of the history of Webster, but one that is not clearly known to me. Two prominent St. Louis businessmen of the 1890's lived in Webster. They were Charles Salveter and Henry Salveter. Mabel Salveter Clayton had been a life long resident of Webster when she died in 1970 at the age of 97. She holds the record for length of membership, 84 years, in the Webster Presbyterian Church. People still refer to the house where she lived on Elm Avenue near Swan as "The Old Salveter Place". Ruth Salveter Cushing was a regular recitalist in the Women's' Choral Club, and the Jessie Gaynor Club in the 1920's. Of course, my grandfather Theodore C. Salveter, Sr. bought a house on Sunnyside near Summit in the 1920's, and raised my Dad and Aunt Helen there. Earl Salveter was my Dad's age, and lived in Webster when we did. He was a very successful businessman, and president of Woerman Construction in St. Louis. He had also been elected Mayor of Webster. So my roots go deep in Webster Groves. My daughter Paige worked in Webster at the Epworth Children's Home and subbed in the Webster Schools. She was the Director of the Webster Hills Methodist Church Activities Center. Her former husband, Dan Cotta, grew up in Webster, and he and his four brothers and sisters graduated from Webster. His parents, Glen and Carolyn, still live there at 117 Waverly Place.

1946, Skip and Charles with Harold and Albert Smith.

Skip, Charles and Dad with Smith kids and gang-1946

Mom and Skip at 548 Summit

CHAPTER EIGHT

•Education•

I have already mentioned that I started 1st grade in Mayfield, Kentucky at the Washington Park School, and attended another grade school there for 2nd grade. When we moved back to St. Louis I went to third grade at Belleview School in Richmond Heights, Avery in Webster Groves and Lockwood in Webster Groves. I had gone to 5 different schools in my first 3 years. I'm sure that no educator would recommend such diversity for a young child. At Lockwood I finally gained some sense of stability in my school life. Of course, I had also lived in 6 different places during this time. This probably explains why I am such a disturbed person today, today, today.

A. LOCKWOOD SCHOOL

For the most part I have nothing but wonderful memories of Lockwood School, which is located near Big Bend and Newport. The teachers there were all loving, and even though Mr. Downs was a stern principal, he was always fair. You see I got to know him pretty well, because I got sent to his office quite a bit in my four years there. He had a big paddle, and in those days they used it. So I would get spanked at school, and then again at home. Back then most parents backed the teachers and principals in the discipline of their kids. Today's parents all too often undermine the teacher and school, and are constantly threatening and suing. The kids are the big losers. When I raised my kids, Teddy, Tony and Paige, I let them know I expected them to mind or catch it from me.

Webster Groves' student population dropped after I moved away, and several schools were closed including Lockwood. A private outfit bought it and made a private school out of it. It's called The College School. Many St. Louis people who didn't want to send their kids to St. Louis public school have enrolled their kids there, and it has been quite successful. I still like to go and look the old place over. So many memories.

I discussed the annual Play Day which was a big event, and the daily recesses, and school yard play including softball, soccer and bombardment. There were the school yard fights, and the school assemblies. Mom and Dad were active in PTA, and they would put on crazy shows. I remember Dad and several of the other fathers wearing grass skirts with coconut shell bras, and doing a hula dance.

We did our own shows, and I remember such starring roles as a shepherd in the Christmas pageant, a sunflower in a school play, and a Mexican guy in a Latin production.

Like most boys I did not like girls. However, in the 6th grade my attitude began to change. This sudden interest in girls got me in trouble more than once. A few girls even started to show an interest in me. At Christmas time the choir, that was made up of 5th and 6th graders, put on a big program for all the parents and other students. It was during rehearsals for this that I was smitten with Margaret Schuhay, who had a beautiful voice, and sang solos. That night, after the program, and as we were putting our stuff away in the music room, I could not resist the urge to kiss her, so I did. She seemed to like it too, but even so, the next day Mr. Downs and his paddle awaited me in the principal's office.

Mistletoe at Christmas time presented what appeared to me a legal license to kiss all you want to. All you had to do was hold some over the girl's head, and it was your right to kiss her. This worked marvelously well, and one day at school I went on an absolute kissing frenzy, me and my mistletoe. It was great stuff. As it turned out, the teachers and Mr. Downs took a somewhat different view of my legal interpretation, and I was not only paddled but sent home for the rest of the day. I have to tell you that it was worth it, although I never understood why the girls, who did not complain, were never disciplined. Back then no one could ever imagine a girl to be so forward and bold.

Mrs. Moore was my homeroom and main teacher in the 5th and 6th grade. I dearly loved her. Our room was also the library. Even though I wasn't the greatest student, I loved to read, and before I left Lockwood I had read almost every book in our library. One of my favorites was Jack London's "Call of the Wild". I continued to read a lot until I was in the 9th grade, when I developed severe headaches. It was discovered that I would need glasses. This was a terrible blow to a sports active kid like me. The eye doctor said it was from all my reading, and if I didn't cut back I would ruin my eyes, and have to permanently wear glasses. That was enough for me. I stopped reading anything, and as a result became a very poor student from then on. My eyes got no worse.

The thing with Margaret Schuhay never worked out. The first real gut wrenching love of my life was Patsy Taylor, a girl who was new in school in the 6th grade. I fell hopelessly in love. I mooned over her so much I felt queasy in my stomach. She wasn't just pretty - she had this something. Today we would call it "sexy". I'm not sure what we would have called it back then. The problem was that I wasn't the only guy who felt this way about her, and my relationship with several of my good friends was becoming strained. One time I was finally alone with her in the cloak room, and kissed her. A couple of my chums showed up and this terrible fight ensued. Mr. Downs was not sympathetic, and I didn't mention the kissing to him. I knew his views on that subject. I'd just take one whipping for fighting.

The whole thing came to a head one day after school. The school was going to show a regular movie in the gym at night. It was a first opportunity to have a "date". I asked Patsy to meet me there and sit with me. The problem was that five of us had asked her, and she couldn't decide. We met on the car ramp that led from the playground to the street. Five guys, Patsy, and a couple of her friends. The problem was stated, the solution was not. First we tried to talk it out. One of the guys dropped out when it became obvious that Patsy wasn't really too interested in him. Now there were four. Nobody budged. There was only one thing to do. We would have to fight to see who would get the date. It was like a joust in the Middle Ages where the knights went at each other for the favor of a lady. Remember Camelot? I was no stranger to fighting. However, this was probably the most important thing I ever fought over. When it got right down to a fight two of the other guys dropped out, so it was just me and one other. I whipped him pretty quick and claimed my prize. I should mention that except for the twins, Harley and Arley Andrews, I was the biggest guy in grade school. Fortunately for me, Harley and Arley never made a play for Patsy.

By the time the big night came I was so excited I thought that I would explode. I met Patsy at school. We selected our seats. The lights went out and the show started. I nervously held her hand, and she gave me these looks with her great big, dark eyes. I thought that I had died and gone to Heaven. There was a problem. Patsy wasn't too interested in the movie. (How could she be sitting next to me?) She was chewing bubble gum. She would blow a bubble, take the gum out of her mouth, and put it close to my face to show me. She kept doing this. Suddenly I realized that the smell of the bubble gum was making my already nervous stomach nauseous, and I got sick to my stomach. I bolted away from her and out of the gym. I refused to throw up at school, so I started running home. It was about five blocks to my house. With me out of the house my mother was having a ladies bridge party. It was lovely, and she had planned it for sometime. She and the other ladies were quite shocked as I burst through the front door and headed up the stairs toward my bathroom. I didn't make it. I had held it all that way, but I threw up all over the stairs and myself.

My relationship with my mother and Patsy Taylor was never the same after that. The romance was over. The thrill was gone. For years the smell of bubble gum would make me ill. Who knows where that magic evening would have led if only I had a stronger constitution? This was 1948. I'm sure that I was ready for Junior High.

When I was in 5th grade, my brother Charles started kindergarten at Lockwood. I used to go down to the first floor and watch him play with clay and toys through the classroom door. I felt very protective of him. He was in first grade when I was in 6th. He was lucky to have a big brother around to look after him. He and I were never in school together again. It's a big responsibility to look out for your little brother at school.

6th grade class, 1948. Skip Salveter, front row right. Patsy Taylor to his right.

B. WEBSTER JUNIOR HI

After being one of the top dogs in grade school, I moved on to Webster Junior High in the Fall of 1948. Junior High back then was next to the High School on Selma Avenue. This meant that not only did I have to deal with a lot of new 7th and 8th graders, there were lots of big high school guys around too. It made me feel pretty insignificant. I went from being one of the big guys to being among the littlest. A whole new pecking order had to be established. There were a lot of fights, and near fights those first few weeks getting that done. My first fight in Junior High was with Tom Bowman. He was loud and obnoxious, and tried to push me around. If I had let him, my career there would have been miserable. He calmed down considerably after that, and wasn't too bad a guy.

To tell the truth, my junior high years were rather unremarkable. We had to learn how to juggle going from class to class each hour. Physical Education classes were a new thing, and so was showering with 50 or 60 guys, all self conscious about their bodies. We had to have white socks, white shorts, a T-shirt, tennis shoes, and a jock strap. I don't remember having a jock strap before 7th grade. There were no inter school sports at the junior high level, but we did have intramural basketball after school.

I found myself becoming increasingly shy around girls. It was a very awkward age. The neighborhood gang still did all the stuff we normally did, and life went on a lot like it always had. Before I knew it I was ready for high school. The question was which high school? I had visited Principia one day in 8th grade, and liked it very much. A mysterious donor made it possible for me to start high school there rather than Webster. I wish that I could remember more about Junior High. I wonder why I can't? Am I suppressing something? Would hypnosis help?

C. Principia

I started Principia in the Fall of 1950. It was located at the corner of Page and Belt in St. Louis. This was the cite of the original school founded by Mary Kimball Morgan in 1897. It is a private school for Christian Scientists, grades K through college. The college is located at Elsah, Illinois. The grade school was called the "Lower School", and the high school the "Upper School". It is for boys and girls. Most of the upper school students were boarding students, and came from all over the world. I did not live on the campus, but commuted each day. We were known as "day pups". I never liked that term. The lower and upper schools were moved to a new campus around 1962 in Town & Country. The neighborhood around the old school campus had badly deteriorated, and was no longer considered safe. The St. Louis YMCA bought it.

Principia was a very expensive prep school, and the reason I got to go there is covered under the chapter on sports. I usually took the streetcar to get from Webster to Principia, and that required at least three transfers each way. I spent a lot of time on the streetcar. Occasionally I would catch a ride with another student's parents. Being a prep school we had to look "preppy", so there was a strict dress code, and a lot of rules and regulations. It seemed pretty strict at the time, and I remember breaking the rules every good chance I got. They even had rules against masturbation, and I always wondered how they enforced that. Since I didn't live in the dorm it was pretty hard to enforce against me.

On Monday, Wednesday and Friday the boys had to wear a suit and tie. On Tuesday and Thursday you could wear a sweater and tie. The girls had to wear skirts or dresses. The level of education was far above public school, and there were many very bright students. Lots of my classmates went on to Harvard, Yale, Cornell, Princeton, and a host of very good schools. Many went on to Principia College, which itself is an outstanding liberal arts college. A lot of my activity at Principia centered around sports, and is covered in that chapter.

Except for sports, my early high school years were much like Junior High, not memorable. At Principia we also had chapel, and convocation once a week. This further helped us to become proper young men and women. I also discovered that they were excellent opportunities to get to sit next to some girl you were interested in. I don't remember any love interest in 9th grade except Carol Falstich. She was pretty, and a very accomplished competitive roller skater. Chapel and convocation also gave you a chance to goof off, giggle and otherwise be disruptive. I'm sure that some of the programs were worth while. Who would know?

I had started to learn to dance in Junior High at Webster, at Fortnightly and other programs. We also had formal lessons at Principia where professional dance instructors would give group lessons to us after school. One problem in 9th grade was that a lot of the girls were taller than the boys. The problem was exacerbated when you had to dance with a taller girl. Some of these professional teachers were probably with Arthur Murray Studios, etc. The female instructors were usually good looking women. They would grab you and give you personal instruction. The hormones of a 14 year old boy are easily disturbed in such a situation. I vividly remember one of them trying to teach me the Rumba and the Samba, and making all those provocative moves. I hated dancing class.

It seems that at Principia there were a lot of school dances, so we got to practice what we learned. Of course, that was hard to do when the boys congregated on one side of the room and the girls on the other. That problem was solved at some of the dances when you were given a "dance card" for the evening. The card specified who you would dance with during each song. Sometimes you would get lucky, and there would be a lot of pretty girls on your card. Other times you would seem to get more than your fair share of "wallflowers". If your luck was really bad, you might feign an illness to get out of a dance. You had to try not to be too obvious.

There were a lot of rules associated with dancing at Principia. It seems that the older you got the more they applied. The school encouraged dancing, but it wanted to discourage what it might lead to. Therefore, there had to be a least 6" of space between the dancers at all times. No touching. The chaperons were kept very busy trying to mingle among the dancers to monitor the 6" rule. If they caught you violating the rule you would get a solid tap on the shoulder, and a stern glance. If the problem was considered bad enough, the girl involved would get a demerit, and there was a whole system set up for penalties for demerits. No kissing, no body touching, no inordinate displays of affection were allowed. As I recall, hand holding was permitted. Compare all that to today's teenager, and you can see what a difference there was. Of course, this was a private school, and the faculty had a bigger responsibility. Especially with the boarding students in their care. Things were looser at dear old Webster Hi.

D. Back To Webster

I went back to Webster for my Sophomore and Junior years. They too were unremarkable except that my parents divorced, and so it was just Charles, Mom and me at home. That divorce seemed to turn our world around and upside down. Mom had to go to work, and money was always a problem. We had been poor before, now we were poorer. Dad wasn't around much. Charles and I were left on our own a lot. I became the "man of the house" at 14. I had to raise myself, and my little brother.

When Dad left so did the car. We either walked or took a bus. Not having a family car as a teenager in a place like Webster was traumatic. We were always dependent on someone else. Mom did the best she could, but it was a real problem for me. When I was 16, and got my driver's license, there was nothing to drive. I had to double date with other guys who had a car. The whole thing messed up my social life at school.

Life as a teenager had its patterns. Get up. Go to school. Go to practice after school. Come home. Eat dinner. Sometimes study. Go to bed. Now each one of those days was full of growing up and minor crisis. A lot of times Charles and I would get home before Mom, so she would have left instructions about what we were to fix for dinner. We opened up a lot of cans of "Dinty Moore Stew".

One of my friends, and a guy I played football with, was Carl Elster. His parents were pretty well off, and he had a brand new car as soon as he was 16. He and I lived across town from each other, and in different worlds. We used to hang out together and ride around in his car. Carl was a little bigger than me and pretty tough. He would intentionally get us in fights by mouthing off to people in other cars. One time he and I drove to downtown St. Louis. Carl thought it would be fun to give the drunks, homeless and winos problems. Fortunately there weren't any around that night. I was not always proud or comfortable with what Carl liked to do, but it was a macho thing so I sometimes went along with it. Peer pressure is tough when you are a teenager.

In study hall he and I developed "spit wad" basketball which we would play along with other stuff to keep us from ever actually studying. In our Junior year it was decided to try to combine one of the boys and girls physical education classes. The problem was what do you do? You can't play football. So it was decided that they would teach us how to square dance. The first day of the experimental co-ed gym class was very awkward. We were in the girls' gym all lined up around it against the wall. Coach "Bear" Bryant was our football line coach. He was big and mean. He was also out of shape, and didn't look too good in his T-shirt. He and the girls' coach got out in the middle of the floor to demonstrate some of the square dance steps to us. Carl and I were having a very hard time trying not to laugh. You know the feeling. Pretty soon Carl let out a muffled giggle. That was all coach needed. He rushed at us, and we both flattened against the wall. Fortunately for me he went for Carl. He grabbed him by the shoulders, lifted him in the air, and smacked him up against the wall. We were scared to death. He "explained" how we better get serious and other stuff, and not be snickering. Then he let Carl drop. We paid close attention after that.

Once in a study hall, coach Bryant caught Nancy Haase talking, and he had her lean against the wall the rest of the class with only her finger. He was a mean sucker, but underneath one heck of a nice guy.

After football was over, and on a Friday night after a basketball game, Carl and Dave Tuttle drove to Nebraska to a farm his folks had. They messed around all weekend, and drove back on Sunday. They never slept. On the way back Dave was driving Carl's Mercury, and Carl was asleep in the back seat. Dave fell asleep at the wheel, and went off the road into a deep ravine. Dave was hurt, but Carl was killed. He was 16 or 17 years old.

Carl's death had a profound affect on everyone. It especially bothered me, because he was my friend, and we played football together. Carl was bigger than me, a better player, better looking, had money, a car, family. I always envied him and wished I could be like him. In my mind he had it all. Now he was dead. This guy that I thought was indestructible was dead. I didn't know what to make of it. I had never experienced death like this. I was in deep grief and mourning. I learned not to be envious of anyone. You never know what would happen.

For a long time I blamed Dave Tuttle for Carl's death, and hated him for it. I even got in a fight with him, and knocked him down the front steps of the school. Time eased all that pain and anger but when my son Tony was killed in 1990 some 38 years later, I thought about Carl's death again and my feelings toward Dave. I realized that I had been wrong to have blamed him. They were both at fault for driving without any sleep. It could just as easily have been Dave who was killed. But most importantly, I realized how terrible Dave must have felt about it. To carry that guilt over his friend's death. I felt like such a jerk. In 1994, I attended the 40th Webster Groves reunion of the class of 1954. I hadn't seen Dave Tuttle since high school, but there he was. I finally took him aside, and told him all about how I had felt, and asked him to forgive me. He told me about the hell he went through after Carl's death, and of the very few people who gave him any support. I'm glad we had a chance to share that. He told me that Carl's parents never really recovered from Carl's death, and both died at a fairly young age of grief. I can certainly relate to that. Dave died of a heart attack in 1999.

There were no "Crips" and "Bloods" in the '50s, at least not that I was aware of. We had our fights, and some of us thought we were pretty tough, but by comparison to what goes on at some of today's schools, our world back then was like a Sunday School picnic. If there was any drug use in the school I never knew it. A lot of the kids smoked, but only the losers did it publicly. Booze was always a temptation, and kids were always sneaking it from their parents stock. I don't ever remember it being around our house. I know that my Dad would have a drink, but it was never a problem. I think that he did a lot of it when he was in school, and before he got married. Christian Science did not allow for alcohol, so that put a damper on it. Mom didn't drink.

I remember the first time that I got drunk. It was in 1952 after football season, and I guess sometime around Carl's death. Jim Krebs was almost 7' tall. He was a senior, and I was a junior. He was the star center on our basketball team at Webster. He almost led the team to its first State Championship. They were undefeated when they lost to Cleveland at State in Columbia and ended 28 - 1 for the year. He was my friend. We both had red hair. He was an All American for SMU and played for the Lakers in the NBA.

Anyway, "Kreber's" parents were out of town, so he had a little party at his house for a few guys, and I was invited. I started drinking beer and other stuff, and got smashed. I had gone over with Dick Bell, and at 2 a.m. he dropped me off at my house. It's a wonder we made it without a wreck. I didn't want to wake Mom, however I was singing loudly enough to rouse all the neighbors. I felt so good. I stumbled up the walk to the front door. I didn't need to worry about waking Mom because she had never gone to sleep. She always waited until we got safely home. She met me on the front porch, and when she realized my condition, proceeded to go nuts. I will never forget her screaming and crying and saying "My son, my son, what have you done? What have you done?" She even accused me of being drunk, and ruining my life. I was 16, and assured her I was not drunk. I really did feel bad that I had upset her so. I guess all of this surely woke Charles up, but I don't know if he remembers it or not.

I told her I was fine, and I was going to bed. Before I got to the top of the stairs I was not so fine, and I spent the rest of the night making love to the toilet. I learned my lesson for a while, and the rest of my high school career was pretty much alcohol free.

I seemed to have an identity crisis my junior year. I played football, so I was a "jock", and that was good. However, my parents were poor, I didn't have a car, and so my social life was a dud. At Webster the coolest thing to be was a "Socie". This was short for socialite or one who was part of the "with it" or "in" crowd. You were "neat" if you were a socie. Now if you were popular or a jock or extremely good looking, you were probably okay. I was just not sure where I fit in, and so the identity crisis. Sometimes I would find myself drifting from group to group.

Some of my friends from the neighborhood, and their friends were clearly not socies or jocks, or popular. They were just guys. Now I liked them, sort of, but I didn't always want to be seen with them. Some of these outcasts belonged to a loose organization known as the "Black Gang". I'm not sure where the name came from, but a lot of them wore black leather jackets, and tried to act like the "Wild Bunch", the old Marlon Brando movie. Of course you remember "The Fonz" on Happy Days. That character, and others like him would have looked like the Black Gang. So I became sort of a member. I said I was a member, but I never had a black leather jacket, or let my hair get long and greasy and slicked back.

There was peer pressure from every direction. I was not a good student, but I didn't think I was stupid. In fact, all through school my teachers and counselors said I was quite bright. I just "didn't apply myself". Well part of that was because I didn't want to ruin my eyes by studying, and part of it was because of the Black Gang. You see, you couldn't be a true rebel if you were making good grades. Anything above a "C" was viewed with suspicion. In fact it was best if you were flunking or on probation. If I ever did accidentally make a good grade in something, I tried very hard not to let certain people know anything about it.

I made an "A" in Business Law, and the word got out. I had to explain that it was an accident, a gift. Secretly I was pleased, and my Mom was sure I should be a lawyer. I really don't know how I got an "A". I got B's in Algebra and Geometry, and that really freaked them out. But I made up for it by getting straight "D's" in Spanish from Senorita Dowd.

Poor Senorita Dowd. She was a frazzled old maid teacher who looked like she just barely made it through each day. Sometimes she would leave the room right in the middle of class in a panic. I believe that she was either snorting something or, having a quick smoke. Who knows? I'll never forget the first day of class as she was reading our names off. When she realized that I was Dad's son, she seemed depressed. He had been her student too, and was every bit as bad as I turned out to be. "Like father, like son". She was depressed. I don't know who she liked least, me or Dad. It was not an easy choice for her.

I just couldn't get Spanish. Not that I tried that much. I just didn't get it. She took it personally. Like a lot of Spanish teachers she went to Mexico each year. Her room had shelves full of little trinkets she had picked up on her annual summer trips to Mexico. She was very fond of all of them. One day before class, which was just after lunch, another guy and I were tossing a football around in the room. He made a terrible throw, I missed, and the ball crashed into one of the shelves sending little Mexican stuff everywhere. About that time she came into the room. When she saw what had happened, she went ballistic, and I think had a nervous breakdown right in front of the class. She grabbed her purse and headed out for a smoke, a snort or whatever she kept in the bag. We never saw her again the rest of the hour.

I felt so bad, I actually cleaned the mess up, especially the broken glass. I don't know if she ever knew who did it , but I'm sure I would have been one of her 3 guesses. I never volunteered that information, and we were always more careful throwing the ball or anything else after that.

I had no great love life my sophomore and junior year. Of course there were some girls I would have killed for, but I never had the nerve to ask them on a date. So no serious relationship ever developed. There was one girl in my history class with Mr. Shelton who I got pretty friendly with. Her parents both worked, and she kept inviting me over to her house after school. I got the idea, and wanted to go but I was secretly scared to death. What a dope! But this was typical of the age. All you thought about and talked about was sex. Some guys even made up some pretty good stories about all the sex they were getting. Some guys really were getting it. Most weren't. Me, I talked about it, and when I actually, maybe had a chance, I got cold feet or something. What was I afraid of?

E. Principia Again

I went back to Principia for my senior year. I still had to take a bus or streetcar occasionally, but most of the time I rode with my best friend Jim Singer and his Mom. Jim lived in Kirkwood and was in my class. His mother worked at Principia. I was sort of on their way to school. Jim was on the football team, and so our schedules were the same in the Fall. However, he was a diver on the swimming team in the Winter, and on the track team in the Spring. I was on the basketball and baseball teams. Jim had a light green 1948 Chevy convertible. We had a blast in that car.

We were very close, and Jim's parents became like a second family to me. I don't guess that I was ever grateful enough for all they did for me. Even though Jim went to the University of Colorado, and I went to Drury, we stayed in touch, and saw each other at holidays and in the summers. When I got married in August of 1957, he was my best man. His Mom passed away after we were out of college, and later his Dad moved to Springfield. I sort of watched out for him. His Dad had been the swimming coach at Cleveland High School for a long time. Jim and his family visited us in Springfield from time to time. His Dad died in the '70s, and I handled the estate. I never saw

Jim again, and no one knows where he is. I feel that he was upset with me over the estate, but that is only a guess. I hope that one day I'll be able to find him.

School at Principia started with two weeks of football at the college campus at Elsah. When that was over school started for everybody. The first week of school we were on the team bus coming back to the campus. As we pulled in, I noticed this attractive girl walking by, and I said to the guy in the seat with me, "Do you see that girl? I don't know who she is, but I'll bet you a dollar I can get a date with her before the week is over." He took the bet. Little did I know that her brother was on the football team, and was sitting behind me when I said it. I was pretty embarrassed when I found out, but I won the bet.

The first social event at the school was an "Icebreaker Dance and Party", and I got her to go with me to it. Her name was Ginger, and her brother was Charles. We hit it off pretty well, and before long we were going steady. Their family was of French-Indian descent, so she was very dark and very pretty. She also had a great voice, and sang a lot of solos in choir and musical productions. We were in choir together. She was first string on the girls basketball and field hockey teams, so she was a jock too. She was on the Girls' Board, Girls' Sextet, and in "Tony Beaver" with me. Besides all this she was probably a straight A student.

Ginger's parents lived in Chase, Kansas, and were in the oil business. They owned Stag Drilling Co., and other businesses. When they would come to town they would always take us out to eat at the Chase park Plaza or some other fancy place. They seemed pretty well off to me. Big old Charlie would eat two steaks. What more could a poor boy have asked for? The first semester rolled by, and everything was great except the strict rules that only allowed for hand holding were driving me crazy. We needed more, and of course we did all the sneaking around on campus that we could. She even got some demerits. Obviously I had become a bad influence on Miss Perfect.

Singer was dating Phyllis Ling, a California girl, and we devised the perfect plan. It was possible for a boarding student to check out for the evening on a weekend in the care of the parents of a Day Student like me. I talked Mom into asking the school to let Phyllis and Ginger out in her care for the evening. Mom was a pretty good sport about it for a while. The deal was that once the girls got to our house she was to spend the rest of the evening upstairs in her room. She was not to come down under any circumstances.

Meanwhile, Jim and I had carefully plotted where each of us would be. We had the lights off downstairs, the old 45 record player cranked up playing soft music. There was the couch in the living room, and a day bed in the dining room. The evening was going perfectly. Well pretty much. The girls weren't quite as enthusiastic as we were, but it was okay. We were definitely beyond holding hands.

I guess the pressure was getting to Mom. No telling what she thought was going on down there. Finally she came to the top of the stairs and said, "Skipper, what's going on down there?" "Nothing Mom, go back to your room." A while later, "Skipper, you better turn some lights on down there right now!" "Okay Mom, we will. Go back to your room." Finally she could stand it no more, and announced that she was coming down in 5 minutes, and the party was over. I guess she had visions of a pregnancy or who knows what occurring on her watch, and she didn't want to be responsible for that. What would she say to Principia? She had nothing to worry about.

Jim and I had played it for about all it was worth anyway, and we took the girls back to school. I think that Mom rode along. This was the '50s.

Lots of times I would have to stay at school either for a party, dance, program or a game, so I wouldn't ride home with Jim. I had no money to buy dinner. I was just barely making it. I had a couple of friends who were waiters in the school dining hall where the boarding students ate. They would sneak food out to me, and I would eat it as fast as I could in some cold dark corner, hoping not to get caught. Lots of times it would be really cold with snow on the ground. I was like some poor homeless person that they took pity on.

If the evening was real late I would sneak into the dorm, and sleep on someone's floor. It was crazy, and against the rules. Some of the "House Pops" were always wondering what I was doing around there at night. Some of them probably figured it out, and looked the other way. I was there one night when one of the Freshmen had a wet dream (nocturnal emission), and the maid discovered the evidence. You'd have thought that he had committed murder the way they carried on about it. How embarrassing for the kid. How could he control that? They said he should have "purer thoughts", and such things wouldn't happen. Sometimes it seems like that place was on another planet. We were pretty sheltered.

Christmas vacation came, the kids went home, and the school closed down. Ginger went back to Kansas for the Holidays. Every New Years Eve the St. Louis Principians had a party at the roller skating rink next to the Arena across from Forest Park. The Arena is where the professional hockey team played, and where the St. Louis Bombers, the pro basketball team played. Singer and I were without our women, and we decided to get dates to the party. I figured Ginger would never know. Right. A school party, and she wouldn't know.

There was a girl in the class behind me at Webster who lived in my neighborhood on Twining Place. Through the years I would see her at school or walking home from school or just around. I knew who she was, but about all we ever said was "hello". Through the years I noticed that she was getting better looking. Lots of times after

Jim would pick me up we'd drive by her waiting for the bus to go to school. We'd smile at each other. It seemed to me that her smiles were extra friendly. Anyway, I decided to call her and ask her for a date to this 1953 New Year's Eve skating party. Much to my surprise, she said she could go. Her name was Sharon Lee Downen. Now it's Sharon Lee Salveter.

I don't exactly remember who Jim's date was, but I believe it was Sharon's friend Joyce Thornton. Whoever it was, we all went to the party, and had a grand time. I could roller skate pretty well, but Sharon wasn't so good. This caused me to have to hold her a lot, and hold her up. I didn't mind. I thought that she was pretty cute. I guess that she had just turned 16 on December 17th. I was 17. I noticed that I was getting a few curious looks from some of the people there, but it was no big deal. We were just skating, and having a good time.

As you know, it is the custom to kiss your date or somebody at the stroke of midnight to help welcome in the new year. It was just our first "date", and I was going steady with a girl in Kansas, but I thought "what would it hurt?" So we kissed, and it was pretty good. After the party I think we parked somewhere and kissed some more. I definitely liked this girl, but I had to take her home.

We had taken the Holidays off from basketball practice, and got out of shape. It was going to be a shock to my system to do wind sprints, and all those other tortures. However, the biggest shock was that first day back at school. I was looking forward to seeing everybody, and especially Ginger. As I walked across campus I noticed that I seemed to be getting the "cold shoulder" from all the girls I would meet. Sure it was January and freezing out, but this was ridiculous. I went to the girls' dorm to find Ginger, but was advised by the housemother that she wouldn't be seeing me today. Then I figured it out. Somebody had blabbed about the skating party, and this blonde that I had brought to it. Ginger had the whole story.

She and her friends made me sweat it out for a week before I actually got to talk to her about it. I assured her that there was no problem. The girl was just an old friend, a distant cousin who liked to roller skate. My Mom made me take her. She wasn't buying any of it. Eventually she broke up with me, and I was devastated. Did this mean that her Mom and Dad wouldn't be taking me out for steaks anymore?

I discovered that my plight did not go unnoticed, and now that I was a free man, several girls were showing some interest. One in particular was a girl in the class behind me. She was cute, and perky, and from California. Now what I knew about "California Girls" was learned from the "Beach Boys" and movies. I figured that they were all wild and untamed. One did not think that about girls from Kansas or Missouri. Her name was "Dawn". Could anything be more California than that? Well she boosted my ego, and healed my pride, and after several dates and weeks we were going steady. This is when I learned that the female brain does not operate like the male brain. Ginger had dumped me over the New Year's Eve debacle. She had no further use for me. However, that all changed when it appeared that others did.

Before long I was getting reports that Ginger liked me after all, and wanted to get back together. Did I miss something? Meanwhile, I was having fun with Dawn. She turned out to be a "friend", as well as a girl friend. She really cared about me as a person. It was the first time I ever remember having a real friend who was a member of the opposite sex. Of course there was more there than friendship. At the time I thought that I "loved" her. I thought that I loved Ginger too, and a few others. Looking back from a more mature perspective, I'm not sure what it was. I couldn't have been in love with all of them could I? There are things you go through until you find the "right one". Whatever it was, it was very important to me at the time.

Singer and I pulled the off campus thing again only my Mom wouldn't cooperate. We got his Mom to do it. This time I took Dawn to his house in Kirkwood. His mother wasn't much better than mine. There was a green house out behind the biology lab at Principia. Dawn and I discovered that no one ever went there, so it became our special place to rendezvous. The rules at Principia were driving me crazy. She lived in a small women's' dorm called "College House", on the second floor. One night I didn't go home after practice. It was decided that I would climb the back of the dorm, and sneak into her second story window. I was strong and athletic, so I was doing a pretty good job of getting up there, but as I pulled on or grabbed the screen it and I fell with a crash to the ground. It was past "lights out", so all the girls were in bed. The campus was locked up for the night. It was quite a loud noise, and woke everybody up. Lights started coming on. Dawn was laughing at me from her window, and told me I'd better get out of there fast. Then the night watchman spotted me and gave chase. I out ran him, got over the wall, and headed for the nearest bus stop, to make that long lonely ride back to Webster.

The next day the campus was all abuzz about the "intruder" who tried to get into College House. A few people knew the truth. We never tried that again.

Eventually the pressure from Ginger to get back together was beginning to have an effect on me. I was faced with a very difficult decision. To this day I am not sure why or how I made that decision, but Dawn was great about it. Being my friend she wanted what would make me happy. Being my girlfriend she wanted me, but she was willing to let me go if that was what I wanted. It probably would have been better if she would have ranted and raved. She gave me an easy way out and I took it. I felt like a first class heel, and I probably was. We broke up, and I went back to Ginger. I felt damned no matter what I did. It was a no win situation.

Ginger and I got very serious after that, and we even discussed marriage. It was decided that after we graduated in June I would go back to Kansas with her for a few weeks. When we graduated my Mom scrimped and saved and bought me a Smith-Corona typewriter to take to college. Ginger's parents scrimped and saved and gave her a brand new 1954 Buick. She and I drove it back to Kansas, but I'm getting ahead of myself.

As I've mentioned before, my scholastic career in high school was not so great. My grades weren't all bad at Webster, and they weren't at Principia either. They were just real inconsistent. If I wrote a paper for English for instance, I might get an "A" for the paper (content & story), and an "F" or "D" for the grammar. I took 2 semesters of chemistry my senior year that was an unmitigated disaster. Not just because I blew up the lab trying to make matches, but because in reality I failed the course. I needed to pass it to graduate, and fortunately good old Dr. Brown liked football players. I just squeezed by with his help.

There were two blows to my ego at the end of the year. I had pretty much decided to take the Drury basketball scholarship, but I was also seriously thinking of taking the Principia College football scholarship. That ended when they withdrew the offer due to my poor grades. This was the first time in my life that there had been a serious consequence to my goofing off in school. The second blow was when Dr. Remington, our principal or Headmaster, called me into his office for a chat. He had never done that before.

Dr. Remington wanted to know what my plans were after I left Principia. I told him "I guessed I'd go to college". He asked me "why?" The only reason I could give him was because I had this basketball scholarship to Drury. He looked me straight in the eye and said "Ted, don't do it. You'll just be wasting your time and everybody else's. You won't last a week!" This was not exactly a pep talk. What he said made me mad, but I had to admit that he had good reason to say it. But what about my Mom, and all those counselors through the years who kept telling me I had the ability, but just wasn't applying myself? Couldn't he see that deep down inside this goof off jock there beat the heart of a real student? His words haunted me for months after that. Could it be that he was right?

I made the choir. Sometimes there were conflicts between choir practice and football or basketball practice. I loved to sing, but I was shy, and my voice was not trained like most of the other choir members. I hoped no one noticed that I really didn't read the music all that well, and relied a lot on carefully listening to the guy next to me. If he didn't know it, we were in big trouble. Through the choir, and some other things, I was discovering my "softer side". It's very difficult being macho in choir, but I probably could have beat up all the other members.

Two humorous things happened that I didn't mention in the Sports chapter. The boys' locker room was on one side of the pool, and the girls' locker room was on the other side of the pool. There was an old door from the boys' shower to the pool. One day after football practice we were horsing around in the shower. The girls' synchronized swimming team was practicing in the pool. Someone hit me pretty hard, and I slid into the rotten bottom half of the door, and right through it out into the pool area. Imagine the surprise of the girls when this naked guy busts through the door. I was scrambling pretty fast to get back through that hole, with a lot of giggling on one side, and laughs on the other. They replaced that old door with a solid metal one.

When we were in the gym for basketball practice coach told me to get our game uniforms on for the team picture. The photographer was having a tough time getting us to smile. A door opened at one end of the gym, and this rather buxom girl walked from one end of the gym to the other, and out the door. There was dead silence as all eyes were on her. The coach said: "Men, there goes the only girl in school who can lie down at a 45# angle". We all busted out laughing, the photographer snapped the picture, and that moment is memorialized in the 1954 yearbook.

F. Drury College

When I arrived at Drury in the Fall of 1954, the words of Dr. Remington were still ringing in my ears. I wondered why I was there. Drury was a "Liberal Arts" school, "40 acres of Christian atmosphere". There weren't a whole lot of electives for a Freshman. I think I took Freshman English, European History, French, Coaching Football, Physical Education and Introduction to Economics. I had no idea what I wanted to be, but I decided that now might be a good time to start studying a little. I remember that my very first major college test was in European History with Dr. Ernest Jacob. He was a Russian Jew, who had survived the Holocaust. I had always hated history in high school, but I liked Dr. Jacob. He was a warm, friendly man, with a thick European accent. I studied for his test like no other before. I had gone to class. I took notes. By my poor standards, I had given my all. The test was all essay, and it was hard. Even so, I thought I had done great. When we got the tests back in a few days there was a great big red "F" on mine. I freaked out.

Remington's words now reverberated through my being. He was right. I was a total failure as a student. I was ready to pack up and go home. What was the use? Fortunately my pledge father, Rick Wuertz, talked me into not giving up, using some of the old football philosophy. I stayed, and I'm happy to say that I ended up with and "A" in European History. Dr. Remington would not have the last laugh!

My grades in college were on the whole much better than in high school. My big Waterloo was French. Just as Spanish had done me in in high school, French got me in college. It was my only "D". Because of the liberal arts emphasis, you had to take a foreign language. I chose French. Beginning French was taught by Dr. Margaret Kidder, who was the Spanish teacher. She loved Spanish, hated French. Just the person you want teaching beginning students. Early on I happened to make the acquaintance of a senior who was a French major. I believe he knew more French than Dr. Kidder. He would help me study.

I really did try at first. I would do the lesson. Go to class, and proceed to get in an argument with Dr. Kidder, because what she was saying didn't square with what he had told me. She acquired quite a dislike for me, and things continued to go down hill. It was a four hour class, and I managed to get a "C". I would have left it at that, but Drury had this rule that if you didn't take the second semester, you wouldn't get credit for the first. So, Dr. Kidder and I were stuck with each other for another semester. I did much worse second semester, and it was obvious that I would fail the class. I'm sure that she took great delight in flunking me, but I reminded her that if I failed I would have to take it again. When the grades came out I miraculously got my "D". She and Dr. Brown at Principia should have compared notes. In any event, Dr. Kidder and I wrongfully assumed that we were through with each other. It wasn't to be.

Even though Dr. Kidder hated me, and French, she loved Siamese cats. It was her tradition to invite her class to her house to spend the evening once a semester. Since I was part of the class, she had to include me. This is not the kind of evening a young college guy looks forward to, but I needed to go. She not only liked Siamese cats, but she had about five of them. They are evil beasts. They would sit high above me on book cases and shelves, and growl menacingly. I guess we were invading their space. I don't know if Dr. Kidder caused it, but at one point one of the "kitties" leaped down on my neck and back, and sunk her claws deep in my skin. That was enough for me. Years later, and after she retired from Drury, her cats attacked her, and almost killed her. I had nothing to do with it.

When Sharon came to Drury, she took Spanish from Dr. Kidder, and even went on a trip to Mexico with her. Dr. Kidder loved Sharon, and couldn't understand how she could be interested in the likes of me. She was always trying to get Sharon to break up with me. So she remained a thorn in my side. I think that after Sharon and I married, and returned to Springfield, the old girl actually decided maybe I wasn't so bad. I hope so.

Any college student worth his salt has a lot of war stories. Most can't be repeated. I took a Labor Economics class from Dr. Wilber Bothwell. He was a good man but very boring. The class was right after lunch which made it worse. Eventually I decided it was not worth my time to attend. I'm sure I was wrong. Dr. Bothwell always took roll but was in such a fog that he never acted like he knew any of his students. As he took roll he would not look up. My friend Bill Mullis was in this class, and always sat on the back row by the door. When Dr. Bothwell would call out "Salveter", Bill would say "here", and that would be that. I always stood outside the door to make sure everything went well, and then I would leave. One day Dr. Bothwell said "Salveter", Mullis said "here", and for some reason Bothwell looked up and said, "where?" I quickly entered the room and said, "here sir!" He looked dubious, but continued the roll call. A close call indeed.

Dr. Bothwell unwittingly turned out to be my savior. The man loved to talk. Once started, he was hard to stop. He had this strange habit of putting one foot on a chair as he lectured. This would cause his private area to get in a bind with his pants. So he would spend the hour talking and adjusting. The girls were embarrassed, the guys amazed. Here's how he saved me. To graduate from Drury you had to pass an "oral composition". This was a frightening experience, because it was just you alone in a room with three professors. They grilled you to see if you had learned anything while at Drury. It was doubly hard for me because I was finishing in three years rather than four, so I was a junior, not a senior. I knew they would discover I had learned nothing at all. The panel was tough. Dr. Stillings (Political Science), Dr. Gibson (Psychology), and Dr. Bothwell (Economics).

They lobbed a few fairly easy questions at me, and I handled them. Then came a question that left me blank. I had no clue as to the answer or the issue. It was time for a more or less diversionary tactic. I B.S.d around for a while, and then asked Dr. Bothwell a question. He took the bait, and proceeded to go on and on. Eventually the other two got so frustrated they declared the exam over. I passed. Thank you Dr. Bothwell, wherever you are!

One shouldn't get the idea that I had nothing but problems with faculty and administration. Actually I got along quite well with most of them. There was however, a problem with Dr. Clippenger, the Dean of the College. Near the end of my sophomore year I still had no idea what I wanted to do with my life. I guessed that I was a psychology major, with an English minor, but what did that mean? What do you do with a psychology major? One day I walked into the CX, and there were my friends, Mitch Hough and Tom McGuire, sitting at the counter, drinking coffee. They were talking about their future as lawyers. They had always wanted to be lawyers, and would go to the University of Missouri Law School. I was intrigued, and asked them all about why they wanted to be lawyers, and how one got into law school. I had no burning desire to do it, but I thought "why not?" This is how I became "The Accidental Lawyer". If I had not stopped by the CX and had that chat with Mitch and Tom about law school, who knows what I would have become. I was so impressionable. Maybe a dentist.

Drury had a program whereby it would give you a degree with three years (94 hours) study, if you were accepted into medical school or law school. They would count your law school hours (30), toward the 124 you needed to graduate. However, you must meet all the normal requirements in your major, and pass your oral and written comprehensive. Since I was paying my way through school, eliminating my senior year sounded like a good way to save some money. That was a good deal, but I now regret that I missed my senior year at Drury. I was in too big a hurry to grow up. I had not yet realized how precious these experiences were, and the joy of learning.

I had to cram a lot of hours into my junior year to meet the requirements. It was about 20 a semester. I was accepted by St. Louis University School of Law. I was all set, except that Dr. Clippinger, the Dean of the College, had to approve it. He called me in, and after beating around the bush, advised me that he could not approve my program. This was not what I wanted to hear. His main problem was that I was a psychology major, and he felt that wasn't appropriate for law school. He said the normal undergraduate work would be political science, history or business. Things got tense. I have never been one to accept "no" for an answer.

First of all I told him I did not agree with his decision. (Of course I didn't have a clue what you needed for law school and what he said did make sense.) Next, I pointed out that I had carefully read the Drury catalog on the "combined program", and there was no requirement that my major could not be psychology. It looked like Dr. "Clip" was making up his own rules. Then he said he might approve if I would write a term paper on the relationship of psychology and the law. I reminded him that the catalog said nothing about writing a term paper, and as busy as I was I didn't have time. I also reminded him that since I had not yet gone to law school, I had no idea how the law and psychology related. It was an impossible request. He finally relented, and approved my plan. I had won my first case! He was not happy about it, and seemed to hold a grudge toward me for years.

The postscript to this story is that years later when I was a practicing attorney in Springfield, and Dr. Clip had retired from Drury, I received an advertisement in the mail for a book entitled "Psychology and The Law". I sent the ad to him with a short note that he might want to order this book because I knew it was a subject that interested him. I think that broke the ice, and before he died he told me that he had not ordered the book, and was still waiting for my term paper.

I rediscovered beer when I went through rush at Drury. It was hard to ignore. That was what you did at rush parties. Drinking to excess is not something that I condone now. I would not recommend it to anyone. Too much heartache and tragedy have been caused by alcohol. However, what I am about to relate is part of my history, and I can't ignore it. Back then it seemed like a part of normal college life. Drury did not condone drinking. It was against the rules, and anyone caught doing it could get kicked out of school. But it seemed like everyone did it anyway. Tom Watling was the Dean of Men. He took great delight in trying to catch someone drinking in a fraternity house or on campus. He would make late night raids or inspections. He would pretend to be your friend, but in reality we learned he was a rat.

I'm not going to bore the reader with drinking stories. They say that "God watches out for drunks and little children". I don't think it's true, but who knows. The craziest thing that happened to me one school night my sophomore year was the Noel Koelling incident. Noel and I had been playing poker and drinking beer with a bunch of guys in New Men's Dorm. Noel lived on the 3rd floor of Fairbanks Hall, and I lived in the Sig Ep House. When we finished playing, Noel and I climbed out of the window, and took all these quart beer bottles with us to dispose of. We both had an arm full of bottles as we reached the back stairs of Fairbanks. About that time, Wilbur the old night watchman, spotted us, and ordered us to stop. Instead of that Noel threw a bottle at him, and we ran up the stairs into the dorm. On the first floor, near a rec room, and living room, were the house parents quarters of Dr. Jackson. As we ran in, Noel fired a bottle at Jackson's door, and we ran upstairs. On the 2nd floor Noel threw his bottles down one hall, and I threw mine down the other. The dorm was beginning to come alive as we woke everybody up. When we got to the 3rd floor, and his room, we realized I couldn't hide there, so he locked me in his closet which for some reason was in the hall across from his room. He then got in bed and pretended to be asleep.

I could hear the angry mob, led by Wilbur and Dr. Jackson, come up the stairs and begin searching rooms. Finally they got to Noel's room at the end of the hall. I guess they didn't believe he had been sleeping. I'm sure his smelling like a brewery didn't help. They confined him to his room, and everybody went back to bed. But there I was locked in this closet. I didn't want to yell for Noel because then they might find me. I was in some considerable distress. The events of the evening, and the chase had sobered me up, but all that beer drinking caused me to need to use the facilities rather badly. I was in there for hours thinking my bladder would burst, when Noel woke up, and remembered he had locked me in the closet. He let me out, I quickly used the bathroom, and quietly snuck out of the dorm. They never caught me, but poor Noel was put on probation, and confined to his room except for class, and eating. One day as I was visiting him in his room, a bunch of Lambda Chi's assembled on the walk below, and began to taunt him. Noel was a KA, and I was a Sig Sp. He was pretty big, and a forward on the basketball team. We thought about going down, and thrashing a few of them, but then we realized that's what they wanted so he would get kicked out of school. Cooler heads prevailed. Wilbur said he could swear there were two guys, but Noel said he acted alone! Case closed.

In order to help pay for college I waited tables in the Commons. It wasn't too bad a job, but sometimes you had to put up with some flack if you were waiting on one of the other fraternities tables. Once I threatened to take on a whole table full of Sigma Nus. That probably would have been a mistake. Some of the richer students probably thought they were better than those who had to work, but I have learned that although I didn't like putting myself through school at the time, it made me a stronger and better person.

I got demoted to the kitchen washing dishes. We had a big machine, but it was a pretty unglamorous job, and even the waiters looked down on the dishwashers. Cleaning the dirty plates was no fun. Eventually I got fired from the dining hall job altogether. I kept getting the run around on who was responsible for that, but it turns out it was my roommate and fraternity brother Dick Dunn who was the student manager of the Commons. I've never been sure why I got the axe.

I got hired by the maintenance department. This was good news - bad news. The hourly rate of pay was more so that was good, but the work was harder, so that was bad. I got to work outside in the fresh air which was good, but out there all the girls and other students could see you working, and getting dirty, and that was bad. My ultimate boss at the Commons was Dr. Milton Grow, the Business Manager of the college. In maintenance, it was Bill McCrae, the Superintendent of Grounds. He put me in charge of several building projects, and I learned some things. "Mac" was a good guy.

One other job I had at Drury was working for Mrs. Charles O'Connell, the Student Union Director. After my career as a basketball player ended, she hired me to manage the concession stand at the games, and any other special functions. "Connie" was great to work for, but once again I was in the students' public eye feeling like a geek. If there was a way to make an extra buck I did it. No wonder I had no time to study.

After going through rush week, I decided to pledge the Sigma Phi Epsilon fraternity. Our old house was at 1035 N. Jefferson. It was sold to City Utilities a few years ago, and is now a parking lot. For three years that old house was home away from home, and I loved it dearly. All the fraternities were pretty good, each one thought it was best. They were all the same, yet very different too. I guess the main reason I became a Sig Ep was Bill Peterson. Bill was from Marshall, Missouri, and a big blonde headed Swede. He dated my almost sister, Marty Holecamp, when she went to Drury. I had met him the summer before. He was a lot of fun.

Our pledge class was the biggest that year, and Sig Ep had the biggest chapter for a while. It was the newest fraternity. My Dad had been a KA at Missouri, so I felt some pressure to join KA. The guys in my pledge class were a diverse group, but all good guys. They didn't all make their grades, and get initiated. Making good grades to get initiated, and to help the fraternity in its overall grade average, gave me some incentive. I think that fraternities back then were a good thing. It gave you a sense of identity. A place where you belonged. The concept of "brotherhood" did resemble a family. We stood together, and we fought each other too. It was very important to be socially accepted at Drury. All in all my fraternity experience was good. When my brother Charles started Drury in 1959, he became a Sig Ep too.

I have remained in touch with only a few of my brothers. In spite of his canning me, Dick Dunn has remained a good friend. So has Dick Miller, and Glen Cotta. We move on in our life experiences and friendships. People come into and go out of our lives. Very few of them stick. Even so, we have all those old memories we share, and when we do get together, it is so easy to be transported back to that time long ago. I am convinced that some of our most memorable experiences are when we are young and in school. It is a time of innocence, and great anticipation. If I could go back, I would.

Skip and adoring sorority fans-1956.

1956 Sig Ep Toga party, Sharon Downen and Skip on right.

"IT TAKES A HEAP o' workin' to make a script a play." is a statement any of these Drury Lane Troupers will attest to. The "Imaginary Invalid" Argon, Ralph Dickenson, is being consoled in the top picture by his sausy maid played by Sabra Manning. In the lower photo Art Blume, Argon's doctor, and Larry Ahlers, the invalid's brother, watch as Art's son, played by Skip Salveter, proposes to Connie Elmore, the preoccupied daughter of Argon. Janet Massie and Betty Morrow help Dolores Elting and Sabra with their stage makeup in the picture at the left. The set, designed by Director Robert Wilhoit, is being painted by Patty Rosson and Barbara O'Connor in the right hand photo.

G. Law School

I started St. Louis University School of Law in the Fall of 1957, three days after I got married, on Labor Day weekend. I had no idea why I was there. I was just 21, and I couldn't believe I was married. I couldn't believe I was in law school. What had Hough and McGuire talked me into? I wasn't even sure I knew where the school was. It was a lot like my Uncle Bud Oberhaus taking me and Mom to start Drury. All we knew was it was in Springfield. We got lost trying to find the campus.

The first day of law school was taken up by a brief orientation. All the Freshmen were in one room. Before the program started, I noticed that all the guys seemed to know each other, and were talking and joking around. I didn't know anybody. The first thing they did was go row by row, and have you stand up, and state your name, the college you graduated from, your major and your rank in your class. As this went on I felt worse and worse, and hoped they would never get to me. One after another they would rise and say things like "Joe Blow, Notre Dame, Political Science, Summa Cum Laude". I was in a room full of brains, who all seemed to be political science, history, economics and business majors. I also noticed they almost all were from Catholic colleges, and universities. Notre Dame, St. Louis University, St. Benedicts, Rockhurst, etc.

Finally, it became the turn of this scared protestant boy to get up, and weakly announce "Ted Salveter, Drury College, Psychology". There was dead silence. I was so embarrassed. I was exposed as a dope from no where. Why didn't I study harder? I wasn't Summa Anything. Why was I a psychology major? Where is the nearest exit? Then this big guy sitting a few rows in front of me stood up, turned and looked at me, and said in a loud voice, "Drury College? Psychology? Where the hell is Drury College?" Everybody laughed, but instead of feeling worse, I felt better. I knew that they accepted me. I was different, but that was going to be okay. The big guy turned out to be Joe Teasdale. We became good friends, and he became Governor of Missouri.

I'm not making this up. Half of our class flunked out the first semester. I felt badly for them, but it was like looking at the cuts on the board for football. I was really glad my name was on there. I think that those of us who were left were a pretty good bunch. Almost all of that class went on to much success.

My evolution as a student was strange. I had been okay in grade school and junior high, poor in high school, and not bad in college. Law School was definitely the hardest of all, but I did even better. In fact, I was considered to be one of the better students in my class. The school had a rule against working, so you could devote all your time to studying. I had to break that rule because I was married, and putting myself through school. I worked in the St. Louis County Probate Court the three years I was in law school. In the summers I worked construction, and other jobs, because I could make more money. I still did not study very much compared to everybody else in the class, but for me it seemed like a lot.

When you are married, and in school, you miss out on a lot that goes on. My days in law school pretty much consisted of going to class, going to Clayton to work, going home, and studying. Of course I was playing basketball on three different teams, going to Marine Reserve meetings, and a lot of other things. I was busy.

In law school your entire grade depended on what you got on the final exam. The exams usually lasted three to four hours. If you were having a bad day, it was a real bad break. It was too much pressure for a lot of guys to handle. I saw a lot of people just stare at the page. All our exams were essay. Fortunately for me, once I started writing, the bull would flow, and the brain would engage.

Teasdale and I had a running battle to see who could rank higher in the class, while doing the least amount of work. That being the case, I didn't particularly want to help him out. I was frantically studying for an Agency final when he asked me if he could study with me. We had about four hours before the test. It turned out that he had no notes or anything, and knew nothing much about agency. I tutored him until test time. He got an A and I got a B+. The irony of that was unacceptable. Even so, when we graduated I was ranked just above him in the class. Take that Joe!

Our senior year we had our course in trial practice culminating in a mock trial. The jury consisted of a civics class from a local high school. We had a real circuit judge. I was defending a criminal case against Jim Roach and Joe Teasdale. They were the prosecutors. We were given the facts, and had to get people to be the witnesses. Teasdale and Roach knew they would bury me. For one thing, Roach worked at the St. Louis Police Department, and had access to all sorts of stuff, including evidence, and photos from the actual case.

My client was drag racing with another guy who was hit head on by an oncoming car. Both cars burned up, and everybody in them was fried. They charged my guy with murder. In the real case he was convicted.

I felt the secret was to get the right people to be the witnesses. I got a classmate, Don Gunn, to be the Defendant, and got this really good looking undergraduate student from the Drama Department, Faith was her name, to be my star witness. Joe and Jim pulled all sorts of dirty tricks, including the actual grizzly photos I didn't know they had. The case was going badly until I put Gunn on the stand to testify in his own defense. Don is a great guy, but a real character. He would do anything. He strayed off the script a little, and put on a tearful crying scene that no one could forget. He was a riot, and those high school kids bought it. Faith was terrific too, and when the jury returned with a "not guilty" verdict, Don broke down and cried again. It was great. We had done it to Roach and Teasdale. Both were prosecutors for a while in real life.

Gunn's performance in that trial was so famous that we no longer call him Don, but "McNaughton". This was for the old McNaughton Rule on insanity. His insanity saved me in that trial.

Lots of crazy things happened in class in law school. Some are worth remembering. There are no electives the first year of law school. Everybody takes the same courses. I'll never forget my first day in class. Naturally we were all nervous and anxious. What would a law school class be like? The first class was to be in Contracts with Dr. Hector Spaulding. He was a well respected professor who was in his 70s or 80s. He taught full time, and also flew back to his Washington D. C. office each week. A most remarkable man. We all sat there but no professor appeared. No one left. No one knew what to do. Where could he be? You have to remember that St. Louis University is a Catholic, Jesuit school. Finally, in walks old Dr. Spaulding wearing some kind of strange tam on his head, a court jester shirt, three pairs of glasses and strange pants. He wasn't carrying a briefcase full of lecture notes but a lyre. Yes a lyre. We were in shock and disbelief.

He said nothing to us, but proceeded to sit on one corner of his desk. We were in stunned silence, all these Catholic men and women. Then he began to strum the lyre, and sing an Irish ditty about the Pope. It was not a mean spirited song, but there certainly was a lot of irreverence to it. He sang a few more songs, thanked us for attending, assigned the first chapter for next time and left the room. Across the street, and outside our classroom window was a huge Masonic Temple. The irony of it all was too much. My classmates took it all in good stride. I'm not sure why he did it, but he had our attention from then on. We had four hours of contracts both first and second semester. I got an A in both classes, and won the American Jurisprudence Contracts award. God bless Hector Spaulding! The

Pope too!

Dr. Richard Childress was my Constitutional Law professor. I wish I would have paid more attention. Constitutional Law was one of those classes that I decided was pretty much a waste of time. It is true that constitutional issues are pretty rare for most lawyers however, it is still something we should know about. Anyway, Dr. Childress was your typical absent minded professor. He always seemed to be in a fog. He had this crazy habit of sitting in his chair up on the raised lectern platform precariously lecturing and balancing on one chair leg. I would wonder what kept him up. Finally one day it happened. The chair tipped over, and he fell backwards off the platform doing a flip. As he flew through the air and picked himself up he never missed a beat in his lecture, and never acknowledged his wipe out. Heck, I'm not sure he even knew that he did it. This was the same man who went down to a local bar near the school and played pinball machines on his lunch hour.

One of my classmates was an electrical engineer. He had his degree from Washington University. Bob was having a lot of trouble going from the black and white of engineering, math and science, to the perpetual gray of the law. He was a student in trouble. One day the professor called on him to "tell us about this case". We were by now pretty much aware of Bob's problem, and since he had never said a word in class before, we were eager to hear his take on the case we were studying. There was a long and awkward silence. "Well Mr. Snapp, what do you have to say? Tell us about this case". Bob started slowly. We leaned forward ready to catch every word of wisdom this engineer would utter. "In this case" he slowly said, "the Plaintiff is suing the Defendant". The class could not contain itself, and burst into spontaneous laughter. The professor thanked him for his insight, and Bob looked relieved. I don't believe we ever heard from Bob in class again after that. I am sure that he is a patent lawyer somewhere.

Joe Simeone was one of my favorite professors. He has remained a good friend. He even became a Missouri Court of Appeals and Supreme Court Judge. He is a brilliant, but very intense man. A very sensitive and caring man. In Civil Procedure one day he explained something that I did not understand or agree with. By now I was not afraid to speak out in class. This was an affliction I had suffered with in high school, and to some extent in college. I asked him to please go over that again. He did. When he finished he asked me if that explained it. I wanted to say yes, but in fact he had only made it more confusing. So I said "not really". So he gave it another try. I could tell that the rest of the class wasn't all that interested in this point. I hated it when somebody else monopolized a class, so when he asked me again if I understood it I should have lied and said "yes". Instead, wanting to move on to something else, I just said, "No, but it doesn't matter". Wrong thing to say. To Joe, everything in the law mattered. He looked at me in disbelief. Then he began to cry. He put his head down into his book, and cried some more. I sat there feeling awful. Finally, he got up, picked up his things, and simply walked out of the room. To this day my classmates do not let me forget the day I made Simeone cry.

Criminal Law was taught by the Dean of the Law School, Norman McDonough. He was a stern man, with a ruddy complexion. One day in class I told him that I could never represent someone I knew was guilty of the crime. He explained to me that it was my duty to represent the man, and not my duty to judge him or decide his guilt. I was to let the "system" do that. I wasn't buying it. I told him that I was sorry, but I just couldn't do it. (This may explain why criminal defense has never interested me) Dean McDonough became very upset with me over this, and pretty much stayed on my back the rest of the semester. Although I am sure that I did much better, he gave me a "C" which did not help my GPA.

When I was about to graduate, he took another crack at me. I told him that I was interested in going to Springfield. No one else in the class was. Yet when inquiries were made to him by some Springfield firms he didn't tell me, but went around to several of my classmates to get them to apply for the jobs. Of course they told me and I was furious. I got one of the jobs anyway, but the Dean was only mildly apologetic.

Don Gunn was filing papers for some lawyer in St. Louis County, and came up to probate court to see me. When I started to introduce him to a co-worker, I completely forgot Don's name. This has been a problem. Don was gracious after he stopped his crying act. I remember Irv Davis lecturing to us before exams. Ed Houlehan living in the stacks of the law library, and acquiring the name of the "vegetable" for his prodigious study. Al Davis and his perfect impersonation of Professor Higgins', "got it?" Roach's trunk full of library books to keep the rest of us from studying, and so many more things. Of course the "Tortfeasors" basketball team, and those touch football games in Forest Park.

I had a lot of good friends in the Class of 1960, and even though I don't get to see them as much as I would like, when I do see them it is as though there have not been so many years gone by. I was and continue to be touched by the love and support that they gave to Sharon and me when Tony was killed. How can I forget Jim and Patti Raymonds driving in the rain from St. Louis, just to hug us at Tony's visitation. Ed Houlehan driving from Kansas City the morning of Tony's funeral to talk with me for a few minutes before he had to be back for court. The letters, cards, flowers, donations from people like John and Gloria King, Dick and Pat Hughes, Henry and Judy Luepke, Don and Sue Gunn, Charlie and Pat Hamilton, John and Mary Lou Hannegan, and so many others. Those Catholic boys have always watched over this Protestant. Maybe those times I went to the Cathedral for mass with John King paid off.

Ted and Tom McGuire 1959, St Louis. The one who caused the accidental lawyer.

1960, St Louis U. Law School graduate

CHAPTER NINE

•Politics•

I don't particularly like labels but if I had to give myself one it would be "conservative Democrat". I firmly believe that most of us inherit our religion and our politics from our parents. We may like to think that we reached our decisions about such matters by careful deliberation and choice, but we don't. Most of us are born into it. We believe that about Muslim extremists, but we don't like to think that about ourselves. We're not much different.

Politics is one of those subjects you aren't supposed to talk about. It can lead to problems. My first recollection of being involved politically was when Truman ran against Dewey for President in 1948. I was 12, and in 6th and 7th grades. I remember wearing Truman buttons to school. I suspect that the only reason I was for Truman was because my Dad was. I'm sure I didn't know much then. Not that I do now. My ignorance is just better educated.

Dad and others insisted that Truman and the Democrats were for the "little guy", "the common man", and it was pretty obvious that we were in that category. My mother's relatives were just as common, if not more so, but those Franklin County Germans seemed to have a Republican streak. So I became a Democrat. Franklin Roosevelt was like a god in our house, and when he died in 1945 it was as if we had lost a member of the family. No one thought that Truman was any good. He was from Missouri. We didn't know whether to be embarrassed by that or not. He turned out to be okay, and for us "commoners", so we stuck by him. It seems to me that Harry is a lot more popular now than he was then. That's what made his upset victory over Dewey all the more sweet.

I have to admit that in 1952, "I liked Ike". Who didn't? It always seemed to me that being for President Eisenhower had nothing to do with politics. He was the president when I was in high school and college, and I was otherwise occupied. He was like a lovable grandfather. My political passions were not stirred to any action. He had been a war hero. The world was safe with him in charge. I could worry about other things. Fortunately, the fighting slowed down in Korea, and stopped in 1953, when I was 17, and a senior in high school. If that war had kept on I suppose there would have been a good chance that I would have been drafted when I graduated. There were young Democrats and Young Republicans at Drury, but I wasn't involved.

When I started law school, and heard about the job opening in probate court, I discovered patronage politics. Judge Hensley was a Democrat, and to get the job I had to be a Democrat too. That part was easy. I also had to get the endorsement of the committee men and women in my precinct, and the endorsement and help of a lot of other people. First, I had to find out who they were. I got it done, and got the job. Now I was firmly obligated to the Democratic party. This was 1957, and I thought that was all I would need to do. I was wrong. The judge had to run for re-election in 1958, and all the court employees (including me) were expected to participate in the campaign. I found myself going to political and other meetings for the judge, speaking for him, passing out cards and literature, and doing whatever else was required. He was a good man, and a good judge, so I didn't mind. It beat studying the law. I graduated from law school in 1960. It was an election year. My old Drury buddy Tom McGuire was running in the Republican primary in Greene County for the State Legislature. I had just moved here. It was August, and Sharon was still in St. Louis finishing up at Washington University. On election day I went to my polling place at Bingham School. To vote for Tom I had to ask for a Republican ballot. This was not easy for me to do. The lady impatiently repeated, "Republican or Democrat?" I hesitated. "Sir, you will have to declare either Republican or Democrat"! It was killing me to take a Republican ballot, but I wanted to help my old buddy Tom out, so I held my nose and softly said, "Republican".

Safely in the voting booth I looked over the ballot to see where I should put my mark for Tom. I couldn't find his name. I looked again. No Tom on this ballot. I went back to the "friendly" lady, and indignantly informed her that there was a mistake, because Tom McGuire's name wasn't on this ballot. With a satisfied sneer she informed me that indeed there was no mistake. The problem was that I didn't live in McGuire's district. I was mortified. But worse than that, I couldn't believe that I had taken a Republican ballot for nothing. Harry forgive me! Tom lost.

I worked in some more local campaigns through the years, and in Jack Kennedy's presidential campaign in 1960. I liked Kennedy a lot, but I have to admit that I had some reservations about his being Catholic. I had schooled with my Catholic friends for 3 years, and I realized there was nothing to fear. I didn't care for Nixon, even though he had been Eisenhower's vice president. I don't think that Eisenhower cared much for him either.

There were a few people in town who I always thought knew what they were talking about. Ray Daniel was an older lawyer, and very active in Democratic politics. He gave me a "hot tip". Most of the hot tips I have received in life haven't worked out. Like John Hannegan's stockbroker brother-in-law's stock tip when I was in law school. A bunch of us invested in Pauley Petroleum. It did great for a while, but eventually we lost our shirts. Ray told me that the next governor of Missouri would be then Lt. Governor Hilary Bush, and that I should get in on the "ground floor". Bush was a Kansas City lawyer.

It made sense. The Democrats controlled the state, and there seemed to be an unwritten rule that to be elected Governor you moved from Attorney General to Lt. Governor to Governor. It was political musical chairs. This was probably 1964. The problem was that nobody explained these rules to Warren Hearnes, who was then Secretary of State. He was a lawyer from the Boot heel, and he wasn't willing to wait his turn in line. Everybody in the Bush camp was pretty sure that Hearnes had no chance. Another lawyer friend, Jerry Lowther, told me that the smart money was on Hearnes, and if I wanted to get in on the "ground floor" I'd back Hearnes.

Two conflicting hot tips. Naturally I chose the wrong one, and backed Bush. I was so confident that he would win that I would call him "Governor". Unfortunately Hearnes upset Bush, and won the primary. He was easily elected Governor in the general election. "Governor" Bush, and Ray Daniel sort of slipped into political obscurity after that, but I was already safely in the Hearnes' camp.

I had been teaching Business Law and Political Science courses at both S.M.S.U. and Drury, and began to get the political bug myself. In 1966, I was happily working for Lincoln, Haseltine, Keet, Forehand

and Springer. I asked them for their blessing to run for the State Legislature. I thought that they would think it was a wonderful idea. Not. They said they were happy with my being involved with community and political affairs, but they wanted me to practice law, and not be a politician.

I was faced with a tough watershed decision. If I ran for office I would have no job. If I didn't run I would always wonder "what if"? I had a wife, and two small kids. I had no money. It was scary, but I decided to run for State Representative from the 142nd District. It was a new district in that the last redistricting had changed boundary lines, but like the rest of Greene County, it had always been a Republican district. I reluctantly resigned from the firm in February or March of 1966, and went out on my own. What a challenge. Starting a law practice and starting a campaign.

I couldn't file locally for this job. I had to do it personally with the Secretary of State in Jefferson City. I put out the appropriate press releases that people were asking me to run, then that I was seriously thinking about it, then that I was close to a decision, and finally that yes, I would submit to the groundswell that was forming and file for office. It is true that some people actually did want me to run. However, these were Democratic officers who were always desperate to get anybody to run in this Republican area. It wasn't easy for them. It was like leading the lambs to the slaughter.

Sharon and the family were not thrilled. She didn't work, and was rightfully concerned about my ability to make enough money to pay my overhead much less support the family. It was a stressful time. I don't know whether I was being foolish or just overconfident. Somehow it all worked out. With hindsight, I'm not sure that I would do it again. Life certainly would have been different in so many ways. We never know what's on the path until we walk down it.

I waited until the last day to file. That increased the drama. I was going to drive to Jefferson City by myself. I had lunch at the old Grove Restaurant on north Glenstone with some political cronies before I left. One of them was Arch Skelton, another lawyer who was an active Democrat, and a few years older than me. His brother is Ike Skelton who has been in Congress for years. Arch informed me that he was going to go to Jeff City to file for Congress against Durwood Hall. I told him that he could ride with me, but that we better get going or we'd miss the 5 p.m. filing deadline. It was getting late, and Arch said we had better fly in his plane.

To tell you the truth I didn't know that Arch was a pilot, but I went along with it. I drove to the airport on east Division, and he went home to get his flying maps and charts. There was a small building at the airport that served as an office, reception and meeting area for pilots and others. I went in there to wait for Arch. I have to say that I did not like to fly, and was pretty apprehensive. I wished that I had just driven. While I was waiting for Arch I was browsing around, and started to read the stuff on a big bulletin board. Then I read this:

"Congratulations to Arch Skelton -

our newest pilot!"

I hit the panic button. About that time Arch showed up and gave the orders to have his plane checked and fueled. I pointed out this note on the board, and asked him how many times he had flown a trip like this or taken someone like me along? He admitted that this would be his first time, but assured me there was nothing to worry about.

I would like to say that the flight was uneventful, but it wasn't. It was "white knuckle" all the way. It never seemed that Arch was in control or knew what he was doing. It didn't help matters that it was a cold Winter day, and the sky was very overcast. Visibility was about 600 feet. I had no choice but to go with him. It was too late to drive and get there on time. When we finally landed at a little airport across the river from the Capitol, I was greatly relieved. We got a cab and drove over in time.

The filing was quick and anticlimactic. There was no fanfare or bands playing as I had expected. We had some time so we went up to look at the House and Senate chambers. They were very impressive, and I could imagine myself in there listening to the debate, and rising to make some stirring speech that would settle the matter for one and all. This was Friday and the legislators had all gone home. We wandered around their offices and ran into Rolland Comstock, a State Representative. He gave us a quick tour, and asked if he could bum a ride back to Springfield. I told him that he might want to reconsider since we hadn't driven but flew up in Arch's plane. I told him I couldn't recommend it. Rolland responded that if it were just he and Arch he wouldn't do it because they were "both scoundrels, and the plane would go down for sure". However, since I was along, "a good Baptist, and pure as the driven snow", he knew they would all be safe. "God wouldn't let anything happen with you on board". It turned out that God didn't let the plane go down, but he sure scared the stuffing out of us all the way back. A postscript to the story was that about a month later Arch completely turned the plane over while landing. He wasn't hurt, but the plane was destroyed.

The final press release was that I had filed. Now I was an official candidate. Fortunately I had no primary opponent, so I was sure to win the August election. I had friends in the Political Science Department at S.M.S.U. who eagerly worked on my campaign. David Heinline was my campaign chairman. Stan Vinning a close advisor. My friend John Lewis was my treasurer. Little by little friends and relatives got involved. I was grateful for the support and enthusiasm. One thing I didn't get much of was money. First of all I was not very good at asking people to contribute to my campaign. I felt it was demeaning, and embarrassing. Secondly, no one gave me any chance of winning, so they didn't want to back a loser. We did get some money from unions, and the normal Democratic contributors, but the campaign was definitely run on a shoe string. I didn't have any money, and I refused to borrow any, and put my family in further jeopardy. So we just made do, and we made most of our own signs.

George Perryman was an engineer, and a Springfield City Councilman. He won the Republican primary, and was a heavy favorite to beat me. He had lots of money, and they ran a very professional campaign. There was a popular old entertainer here by the name of Bill Ring. I remember one of the low points of the campaign was when I was driving in my car, and heard a new Perryman campaign ad on the radio. Bill Ring sang:

"P E double R Y - M A N spells Perryman

He's the man with the plan and a real American. Perryman, that's who!"

My heart sank. I hated it, but I liked it. It was so catchy that I would even sing it. Then my family, Sharon, Teddy and Tony would sing it. That jingle would take over the world. I was doomed. We couldn't come up with a jingle or a slogan of our own. Several of my friends came up with some pretty obscene ones. The best we could do was:

"Ahead with Ted"

Of course that got mangled into:

"To bed with Ted"

I made a lot of speeches and went to a lot of neighborhood coffees. I hit so many school chili suppers one night that I threw up. I decided that I would campaign by going "door to door". This was probably pretty effective, but a lot of hard work. In the evenings I would take Teddy and Tony with me for a couple of hours. They were such cute kids that if the people didn't like me they couldn't help but like them. Tony was three and Teddy was almost six. For the most part the boys were good troopers, but they did get tired, and they did get bored. One thing they did like was the annual Jackson Day Festivities. There were lots of free food, balloons, bumper stickers, buttons and other stuff, and they made the rounds. Sharon knocked on a few doors too, and did her best to be a candidate's wife, but it didn't come naturally to her, and she didn't like it. She has always been very attractive, so I was proud to show her off. I figured that if the voters thought I was good enough to get her, maybe they would vote for me.

I never cease to be amazed at some of the screwball opinions and ideas people have. I would get quite an earful of bizarreness every day. One day I knocked on a lady's door who demanded to know my position on "Daylight Savings Time". Now one thing you quickly learn as a politician is not to take a firm stand on anything until you know how it's going to play. This was an issue I hadn't thought much about, so I was caught a little off guard. Personally I always liked Daylight Savings Time, because it gave me an extra hour in the evening to play or work in the yard. Before I got out on a limb with her I wanted to see which way the wind was blowing. So I asked her what she thought about Daylight Savings Time.

She didn't like it. It wasn't "Gods time". I didn't know if God had a position on how we humans counted time, but I guessed it was possible. But she went on to say that the main reason she was against it was because of her garden. Her meaning was not immediately clear to me so I asked her to explain how Daylight Savings Time was affecting her garden. She looked at me like I was a real dope and said:

"That extra hour of sunlight every day is burning up my garden".

No matter how hard I tried to explain that there really wasn't an extra hour of sunshine each day, she wouldn't be convinced. Finally she slammed her door, and announced that she wasn't going to vote for me anyway, even if I had been against Daylight Savings Time.

It's a funny story, but a very scary one. When you read about the views of some people, and some groups like the "Freemen" or "Branch Davidians" or the various militias, you can see what a large lunatic fringe there is out there. It's not just our country. They are everywhere. The suicide bombers in the Middle East, and elsewhere. The far right or loony left. Education is the key. Get these people to see the broader picture. To think and reason about things. We may never get there, but God help us if we don't.

Elections are always the first Tuesday in November, and by the time the day finally arrived, I was pretty sure I was going to do better than everyone thought. What do you do on election day? Most people say that it's all over by then so just relax and wait for the results that night. I figured I would go nuts if I waited around, so I decided to spend the day at the most Republican polling place in the district. That was Phelps School. I stood out there with people who were volunteering for other candidates. The high school daughter of an attorney was handing out Perryman literature. At first she was pretty hostile to me, but by the time the day was over we were old buddies, and she stopped handing out his stuff. The people that came by were pretty friendly, and I felt like I had maybe conquered the enemy territory.

The polls closed, and I returned to our home at 1837 S. Hampton to await the results. We had lots of family and campaign staff there with us. As the results came in we all carefully watched the TV to see how I was doing. It was bad, it was good and finally they announced that with one precinct yet to report Perryman and I were dead even. That one precinct was the one that I had been at all day. I couldn't wait any longer. A few of us quickly drove to the courthouse where they were counting the ballots in the county clerk's office. I just knew I was going to win because I had been so charming that day at Phelps School. I was very excited. Finally they counted the last ballot.

I did not win. I lost that ward by just 33 votes. That in itself was a moral victory, but moral victories don't win elections. 33 votes is not very much, but it was a loss anyway you slice it. We were all pretty sad. I went over to the party headquarters watch party, and thanked everyone there, and made my concession speeches for TV and radio. I congratulated George on his victory and offered my support. I wanted to say something about that damn jingle, but I didn't figure the time was right.

For the next two years I had to watch the Legislature in action from afar. I had decided I would run again. I had come too close to turn back now. I had done so much better than anyone thought possible that all were encouraging me to go for it again. I remained active, and stayed up with the issues. In the meantime I was also trying to build my practice. In 1967, I formed a partnership with Wayne T. Walker, which lasted until he died in 1990. I had supported my family through it all. Things were looking up. At least people knew who I was.

Things were completely different when I ran in 1968. People now thought I had a chance, so it was easier to raise money. No more homemade signs. The campaign organization had stayed intact, and we were a more polished bunch. Perryman was the incumbent and this gave him a lot of advantages, but it also gave him a record he had to defend. I had kept careful track of his record, and what he had done the last two years. He would still have a lot more money than me to spend, but I was catching up. His big advantage was just being a Republican. 1968 was a presidential year, and Nixon was running against Hubert Humphrey. The Democrats were in disarray over Vietnam and the antiwar protests. The Republicans were a shoe in. Humphrey would drag everyone down with him.

The 1968 campaign was much the same as 1966 except it was more exciting because of all that was going on nationally with the war. People were really interested in politics. I can't remember all the funny things that happened, but we all had these big campaign signs on the top of our cars. "Salveter For Representative" in big red letters. One day as I was driving to the office in the rush hour traffic, I noticed flashing police lights ahead, and the traffic having to go around the car pulled over. As they went by they all saw my sister-in-law, Karen Salveter, pulled over for speeding with the big "Salveter For Representative" sign on top of her car. I waved to her as I went by wondering how many votes that cost me. She sickly smiled and waved back. I didn't stop because then we would have two "Salveter For Representative" signs holding up traffic.

The best way to learn how to do something is to just do it. I was getting pretty good at being a candidate. In 1966, I would be terrified sometimes to get up before large crowds and speak. Now it didn't bother me much at all. I could handle questions and interviews, and I loved being on television. On election day, November 5, 1968, I was still nervous, but I quit campaigning, and tried to relax. I had done all I could do.

The watch party was at our home at 1333 E. Delmar. We had moved there right after Paige was born in January, 1967. The first returns were horrible. Nixon was killing Humphrey, and got as much as 65% of the vote in my district. Even though the early returns had me losing, I knew I had won. I now knew the district so well that I could predict the outcome from very little information. (Kind of like the Networks do on election night) When I announced to the family and close supporters that we had won they were incredulous. How could I say that when the TV was telling us I was behind?

I went to the watch party feeling very confident. There I mingled with the faithful, and did several TV and radio interviews. The news was better. I was catching up. I was pulling ahead. I had won! It was a great feeling. Nothing like it. A night to be remembered. Giving a victory speech is much better than a concession speech. I had won by 750 votes.

The days that followed were a blur. Somehow I had to keep my law practice going, and be a State Representative too. A tall order. I was one of the youngest, if not the youngest member of the legislature at 32. I had a lot to learn. The strain on me and my family would be great.

Soon after the election I went to the Capital for the Democratic caucus. There we decided who would be Speaker of The House, and the other officers. Since we controlled the House we could do that. No matter what fighting went on in the caucus, once it was over we would all vote together. We elected Jim Godfrey from St. Louis as Speaker, and my law school classmate Dick Rabbit, as majority leader. John Schneider, another classmate from St. Louis, was also elected to the House in 1968.

After the caucus I took a two week trip with other Freshmen legislators on a bus around the state. We visited state hospitals, schools, prisons, and other state facilities. It enabled us to see first hand the places we would be legislating about. That was no pleasure trip. It was led by Lucky Cantrell from St. Louis County, who was the Appropriations Committee chairman. He was like a drill sergeant getting us on that bus early in the morning. I learned a lot in those two weeks.

The Holidays of 1968 were great. We had a lot to be thankful for, and it was a pause in the action before the Legislature went into session in January. It was the last time things would be "normal" around our house in quite a while. I learned from Tony, who was then 5, and in kindergarten, that he had gotten his teacher to vote for me by learning how to tie his shoes. He was quite a campaigner at Roundtree as was Teddy. I would miss Sharon and the kids more than I knew at the time.

Warren Hearnes had been re-elected as Governor, and a big inauguration was planned. A Republican was elected to statewide office for the first time in a long time. John Danforth was elected as Attorney General. He and I are the same age. He had graduated from Country Day in 1954, while I was graduating from Principia. He was a Republican in a Democrat state, and I was a Democrat from a Republican district. We got to know each other. He went on to become a very fine U.S. Senator until he retired in 1994.

Inauguration Day was January 16, 1969. It was a very cold, blustery day. A lot of the festivities were to be outside. It was sunny, but only about 20 degrees. On January 8, 1969, I was sworn in. We were all excited about going to Jefferson City. My mother, Aunt Helen and the Schuettes were to meet us there. We were running late trying to get the kids all ready to go. Things were going pretty well until we got near Camdenton, and Tony got car sick. He threw up all over himself, and the back seat of the car. This was not how I pictured life as a prominent legislator would be. We were sworn in in the House chambers by a member of the Supreme Court.

There were parades, bands, speeches, and the swearing in of the newly elected at the inauguration. The Governor, and other state officers were sworn in outside the Capital on a big platform, and grandstands. It was so cold, but everyone bravely sat through it all. After that, Sharon and I went to the Inaugural Ball. I had on my tux, and she an elegant evening gown. A Springfield Newspaper photographer and reporter were there, and took our picture for the paper. It was quite an evening. The main ball was in the Capital rotunda, but there were parties all over the city. Glen and Carolyn Barclay had worked in the campaign, and were friends and neighbors. They came up for it, and I remember that Glen lost the pants to his tux.

After all this hoopla, we got down to the business of making the laws for the State. There was a lot to learn about how the House and Senate worked, and about the issues. I would leave Springfield early Monday morning and get to the Capital before the proceedings started. I would stay there until we adjourned on Friday, and come home. At home I had to spend most of my time trying to catch up at the office, and talk with constituents. There was little time for the family, and this put quite a strain on all of us. My legislative pay did not make up for what I lost by not working. I took work with me to Jefferson City, and when I wasn't doing legislative work, I'd do some legal work. I wish we would have had faxes back then or computers.

The reading was enormous. Every morning I would routinely read the St. Louis Post Dispatch, Kansas City Star, Springfield News Leader and the Jefferson City paper. In addition to that there were hundreds of bills to read, and volumes of material furnished by lobbyists and others. I learned that almost every bill we considered had some secret hidden agenda. You couldn't take anything at face value. Then there were always the political ramifications to each vote cast. How it played in Springfield and how it played in Jeff City were two different things. It was always strange to be part of the majority in Jeff City, and come home to my district, and be in the minority.

I got in with a bunch of young Democratic lawyers who were affectionately known as, "The Hell raisers". So named because they were very bright, but not too reverent. When the days got long or the debates tedious, you could always count on one of them to offer an amendment to bring out some humor. Once during a debate on a bill to allow corporal punishment in schools, an amendment was offered to allow firing squads. I don't know how the voters would view such frivolity, but it helped keep me sane. I was honored to be part of the group. We actually did a lot of good to a lot of bad legislation.

One night there were antiwar demonstrations that got out of hand. A small bomb went off near the Capital, and the State Police and National Guard were called out. Some heads got knocked in around Lincoln University, and the security around us got really tight. It was pretty scary, and I had no sympathy for the students who were doing the demonstrating. They had ruined the Democratic Convention in Chicago in 1968, and their behavior got blamed on the Democrats. I kept my eyes on the gallery.

Doc Groves was a Republican legislator from North Springfield. We sat on opposite sides of the House. They were on the left and we on the right. A lot of the stuff we had to deal with pertained only to St. Louis or Kansas City. So we would just sit back during those debates, and watch them fight each other. One day after lunch we took up a "St. Louis bill". I don't know where Doc had drunk his lunch. Finally a legislator who was not from St. Louis was recognized to speak. He told the body that "he was sick and tired of hearing about these parochial interests". This brought Doc to his feet.

The place got completely quiet because everybody knew and liked Doc, and because he never spoke on a bill. We hung on his every word. This is what he said:

"Now you boys hold on just a minute. I don't care what we argue about, but I think we have to leave the Catholic religion out of it."

That brought down the House with laughter. I don't think Doc ever realized what he said, but he did know that nobody felt like arguing after that.

Every now and then Tony would spend the week with me in

Jeff City. My staff there and the other legislators really liked him, and spoiled him rotten. He wandered from office to office taking full advantage of it. It was great having him there. I always had committee hearings in the evening, and he would go with me. One night we snuck out, and went to see Yvonne De Carlo and a touring Broadway cast in "Showboat". We both loved it.

1970 came, and it was time to file for re-election. By now I was beginning to feel the stress of doing two jobs, and being away from the family. The excitement had long since gone, and all that was left was a lot of hard work. I thought that my first term had gone well. I seemed to be liked and respected by my peers, and I had made many new friends. The local newspaper had remained supportive, and overall I felt I was making a contribution. The thought of another political campaign was not appealing, and frankly I didn't know how I would find the time.

I began to have delusions of grandeur. I saw no reason why I wouldn't be re-elected. I had done a good job for my constituents, I thought. If I could keep winning in a Republican district as a Democrat, what would prevent me from being successful on a statewide race, eventually Governor or U.S. Senator? My thinking was that I should run strong in southwest Missouri, and with my St. Louis ties, I should do well there too. Why not? It all sounded perfectly logical and doable.

First, I had to win in 1970. My victory in 1968 had greatly upset the Greene County Republican party. Even though I thought that Donnegan, Groves, Langsford and Curtis were friends, I misunderstood how the game is played. Their first loyalty was to the GOP, and that meant get Ted. I was targeted, and they would spare no expense or pull no punches. They recruited Dan McGuire, a local Channel 10 weatherman, to run against me. Dan was a friend of mine too, but it didn't matter. He was very popular and everybody knew him.

Not only did they spend an enormous amount of money, Dan knocked on every door in the district twice. He had nothing to do but campaign, and do his TV weather. I was struggling to find time to campaign at all. At the last minute they circulated a sheet of absolute lies about me, and there was no opportunity to respond. My first encounter with Republicans' dirty tricks. I don't know what effect that had on the outcome. SMSU had done some polling on my race a few days before the election, and it showed me getting as much as 60% of the vote. It appeared that I would win handily.

Up to election day we had really nice weather. On election day it sleeted and snowed. The turnout in the district would normally be about 10,000 votes cast. There were only about 7500 votes cast. When I saw that the vote was light, I knew I was in trouble. I knew that the hard core Republicans would vote no matter what the weather was like. I also knew that the Democrats, and independents might just stay home. That's what happened. Even so, I only lost by around 100 votes.

The irony of losing because the weather was bad, and running against a weatherman, was not lost on me. I always wondered just how much influence Dan had up there - old "Dan The Weatherman"!

Was my political career over? I was still young and this was pretty much a fluke. Even so, why would anyone put his future in the hands of something as fickle, and unpredictable as the weather? It didn't matter that I had done a good job. I was tired. I knew that all I had been doing for the last several years was beginning to take its toll on me. It was time to regain a normal life, and get reacquainted with my family. It was time to just devote myself to being a good and successful lawyer.

I ran into Dan shortly after the election and congratulated him personally. I had done it publicly with my concession speech on election night. However, I told him that I was very disappointed in him over the scandal sheet. He claimed not to know much about it. I told him that a lot of people had urged me to sue to set the election aside over all the fraud that had gone on, but that I had decided to just forget it. I also told him that he had been used by the Republican party for the sole purpose of defeating me, that he would hate it in Jefferson City, and frankly wouldn't know what was going on. He took offense to that, and told me he'd do just fine.

Before he had served a year of his term he announced that he would not seek re-election. I happened to see him shortly after that, and he was much friendlier. He said, "You know, you were right. After about the second day up there I had no idea what was going on. That's why I'm getting out. Ted, I'm sorry." It was hard not to like Dan, and I appreciated his frankness and honesty. Still, I have to wonder what would have happened if I had won that second term, and gotten firmly established. There are a lot of "what ifs" in life. We just have to see where the ride takes us.

I never ran for "political" office again. In 1974, I decided to see if the Salveter name still had any voter appeal. I filed for the Springfield R-12 School Board. I had made up my mind that I would not spend one dime on the election, and I would not campaign. I just put my name out there. I made two appearances at League of Women Voters forums, and did a newspaper interview. That was it. The others were spending money, and campaigning hard. I won the election by a wide margin.

Service on the school board was very interesting. I had 3 kids in public school. Sharon had been a teacher before we had Teddy, and I had taught at both SMSU and Drury. The job didn't take as much time as being a legislator, but it was demanding. As the years went on we started having more meetings and projects to the point where I finally decided I had to resign. The other board members were either independently wealthy, retired or had jobs that encouraged service on public boards. I was the only one that had to actually work for a living.

While on the board I attended 3 National School Board Conventions in Huston, Texas, San Francisco and Miami Beach. Sharon went with me to Miami Beach, and San Francisco, and we had great times. In San Francisco, F. Lee Bailey was staying at The Stanford Court as were we. He was there on the Patty Hearst case. I rode in an elevator with him one day. I used to admire him, but after the O.J. Simpson case I have little respect for him or for defense lawyers in general. I guess they are just doing their job, but society sometimes pays dearly for their success. While we were in San Francisco we went over to San Jose and spent a few days with Sharon's sister, Pat and her husband Bob Biesinger.

In Miami Beach I saw my first Dog Race and Hai Li game. There were a lot of retirees there, and although the ocean and beach were beautiful, a lot of those grand old hotels were in a state of decline. Still it was a fascinating place. We ate our fill of "stone crabs".

While I was on the board we had to terminate a non- tenured teacher who turned out to be a menace in the classroom. He lectured the students on a lot of inappropriate subjects. The net result of that was we got sued by him in Federal Court for several million dollars. The case dragged on for a long time, and each time I would apply for a loan, or fill out a financial sheet, I had to show this big lawsuit against me. We eventually won the suit, but it was a pain.

After I got off the board I felt like a big weight was off my shoulders. We didn't know much about the effects of stress then, but now I know that all the pressure of political, legal and public service had begun to take its toll on me. I couldn't handle things like I once had. So when my friend Joe Teasdale asked me to be his campaign chairman for Governor in 1976, I turned him down. I did serve for Jack Schramm in his losing bid for Lt. Governor. I'm not sure that Joe ever really understood my mental anguish at the time. I believe that if I had done that job it might have pushed me over the edge. When Joe was elected Governor the guys that did serve raked in a lot of political benefits, and I couldn't help but think that should have been me. "If you want to play you have to pay".

Now all I'm good for are financial contributions to campaigns, and I'm even slowing down on that. It is a strange phenomenon, but every two years, when the elections come around, I agonize over whether I should run for some office. People are still wanting me to run for Congress or judge or something, and even though I can feel those old political juices start to stir, I know what is involved and how it would disrupt my life. So I go through this mating dance every two years, but never mate. I can't say that I won't ever do it, but it's not likely. I just let another filing deadline go by the other day.

Ted and family-1966

1969 shaking hands with Gov. Warren Hearnes in State Capitol.

CHAPTER TEN

•Religion•

At this stage of my life one of the things that I am most interested in is religion, theology, philosophy and spirituality. I have even thought of pursuing religious studies full time. One of my prime motives is to find the answers to life's difficult questions. What discourages me is that none of those teachers, ministers, and evangelists who are in it full time have any good answers. I believe that in this life we are going to be pretty much in the dark. Just as Paul said, "Now we see as though through a glass darkly". Even though the quest may be hopeless, it seems that some of us are bound to try to figure it out. All this studying, preaching, teaching etc. provides full employment for men of the cloth and religion professors. You would think God would have just told us, and cut out all those middlemen.

My mother was raised Evangelical and Reformed. My dad was raised in Christian Science. When they married she joined his church, and became a devout Christian Scientist. When we lived in Mayfield, Kentucky my dad was 1st Reader in the church. This is as close to a pastor as you get. My paternal grandparents, and my aunt Helen were very active "Scientists". So I was raised in the Christian Science church and Sunday School.

I remember that as a very small boy I loved God with all my heart, and believed that He loved me. One of the first scriptures I learned was "God Is Love". Not only that He loved me, but He was love. That was his nature, and love was the most important thing there was in this life. Deep down I still believe that, but life has shown me that it's not all that simple. There have been too many times when God did not seem to love me or any of His children.

In Christian Science there is a major emphasis on solving problems and healing through prayer. You have probably heard people say that "Christian Scientists don't believe in doctors". What they believe is that Jesus taught us that the power of prayer is sufficient to meet every human need, and that doctors and medicine are not required. This position has created many problems for the church with government and the medical community. Scientists are not "faith healers" in the sense that some Pentecostal, and other denominations might be. It's not just pray and wait for God to work a miracle. It's very complicated. Constitutional issues of freedom of religion are involved when the government requires vaccinations or immunizations, and

Scientists say they should be exempt. A conflict then arises between the duty of government to promote public health and safety, and the First Amendment. Before I could start first grade in Mayfield I had to be vaccinated, even though this was against my parents religion. Sometimes a child might die of some injury or disease that could be routinely treated by a doctor. The prayers or faith of the child or parents were not effective in that case. Are the parents negligent for holding to their religious beliefs? What went wrong?

I grew up without doctors or medicine. There are Christian Science practitioners who can be consulted on serious problems. My understanding is that since God's creation and man is perfect, any illness or condition that would appear to be a reality is not the truth of the situation. Things aren't always as they seem. We were always exhorted to "know the truth". The truth was that sin, sickness and death are not real. The real man is spiritual, like God, and not subject to these negative laws. I must be honest and say that as a kid growing up my interest was in sports and other things, and although I affirmed a belief in this, I never really understood it, or questioned it. "Knowing the truth" always seemed to work around our house. I remember that it was quite a shock to the family when we learned that my aunt Helen Wardan had been secretly taking my cousin Pat to see a pediatrician. Aunt Helen had lost a couple of babies, so I'm sure that she was just covering her bets.

60 years later we are seeing that all mainline denominations recognize the effect of our minds and spirits on our physical health. Most of the complaints that people see doctors about have no physical or "real" basis. They are caused by stress, emotional turmoil or spiritual and psychological problems. The "mind-body" relationship may be "New-Age" mumbo-jumbo to some, but it appears to have a solid basis in scientific fact. But I digress.

When I attended the Methodist church in 7th and 8th grade so I could play on their basketball team, I first realized that everyone didn't pray as I had learned to. My Methodist Sunday school teacher felt it was quite all right to pray for a new Cadillac or other material things. In Science we would know that the truth of any situation was that God would meet our needs, and that we would be in our "rightful place". We would never just pray for God to do something for us. We didn't pray for "miracles". Only for the right order of things to be made manifest in us. I realize that I could be way off on what Christian Science really teaches, and that my memory on this or any other subject in this book could be wrong. What is important is how I perceived it to be, and what compelled and motivated me in my life.

The hardest concept of all to understand is the belief that our physical selves, our bodies etc., are not real, and that a perceived illness of our body is not real. It always "seemed" so obvious that I am in fact here in a physical body, and it does get hurt, and it does get sick. I believe that my essential and eventual nature is spiritual, but right now I seem to be both. Am I a figment of my own imagination? Of yours?

When Sharon and I fell in love, and decided to get married, religion was a serious consideration. I knew that there was no way I would ever convince her to embrace Christian Science. She was raised a Southern Baptist. Her family was active in the church. Her dad was a deacon, and taught Sunday school. I started going to Baptist churches with her when we were at Drury. At the time we became engaged in November of 1956, they were members of the Kirkwood Baptist Church.

No matter what Baptist church we went to, there was an alter call at the end of the service. For a long time it never dawned on me that this question of salvation had anything to do with me. "Salvation" was not a subject that was dealt with in my experience as a Scientist. We didn't think in terms of Heaven and Hell. Eternal life with God was a given. We didn't all grasp God's truth at the same speed, but we were all headed in the direction of perfect "One ship" with Him. I had no concern about my soul.

At some point some of those "Hell fire and damnation" sermons started to have an effect on me. The life I was leading as a college student was pretty wild at times. Maybe I was a sinner in need of forgiveness and salvation. Those alter calls became unbearable. I kept wrestling with what I should do. Being a very proud person, and 20 years old, I could never see myself getting up out of a pew, walking down the aisle, and making a "profession of faith" in front of a bunch of people I didn't know. I certainly would never consent to be baptized, a concept that was totally foreign to me, and to Christian Science.

Then it happened. We were in a service at Kirkwood Baptist Church. I don't have any idea what the sermon was about. All I know is that I was miserable. When the alter call came I was in sheer agony. Before I knew what I was doing, I took a step out of the pew and into the aisle. I don't know who was shocked the most, me or Sharon. I went down the aisle, met the pastor at the front (I think his name was Reverend North), and told him that I was presenting myself as a candidate for salvation and baptism. Another sinner saved!

Sharon and her parents were overjoyed. I'm sure that they had been praying for me to see the light. I felt like a 2000 pound weight had been lifted off of me. This was in the Spring of 1957. I was baptized by immersion by Reverend North shortly thereafter. Why did I do it? What forces were at work within me causing me to take that action? I don't honestly know. I believe and hope that it was the Holy Spirit, and that in that act I found salvation. It's not that I question my salvation. I don't. It's just that I have come to see that the Bible, and the various beliefs people have are so complex on this subject, that if there is only "one right way", it would be hard to know what it is. Frankly I don't believe that God would make something so important so difficult. I just don't believe He is going to zap someone just because they didn't get it quite right. Who gets saved, and why, is one of those questions that won't be answered until we are out of this world. Then we'll probably know.

Sharon and I were married in the Webster Groves Baptist Church on Summit, on August 30, 1957. We were members there all 3 years that I was in law school. I was becoming immersed in Baptist beliefs and customs, but I still thought about things as a Christian Scientist. I would still occasionally go to church with my Mom. I suppose that my mind was getting mixed signals. Still, I was not deeply into it, and really had no time to be.

When I graduated from law school in 1960, we moved to Springfield. I had just spent 3 years with the Catholics, but very little of that rubbed off. I did acquire a profound respect for my Catholic friends, and for priests and nuns. As I would walk across the campus at St. Louis University I would humbly say, "Good morning father, good morning sister", and feel some special stirring in me as I did it. However, I could not accept much of the doctrine and dogma of the church, and to me the Pope was just a man who was the head of an organization, and not infallible, not a spokesman for God. Maybe I was influenced by too many Bing Crosby movies.

Sharon and I shopped around for a church, and finally decided to join the University Heights Baptist Church in 1960 or 1961. We liked Reverend Charles Lunn, and we liked the fact that the church was uniquely "duly aligned" with both the Southern and American Baptist Conventions. We became very active in the church as teachers, and in other ways, such as church plays and programs, vacation Bible school, etc. I was on lots of boards and committees, and even served as Superintendent of the Sunday school. I taught the adult Pioneer class until April of 1995 when I resigned. All 3 of our children were baptized there.

In 1975 we joined Evangel Temple, an Assembly of God church. We made the switch because there were problems in the Youth program at University Heights, and because both Sharon and I had become involved in the "Charismatic movement". Mainline Baptists pretty much rejected the idea of "speaking in tongues", and other evidences of the Spirit in a believer's life, so we felt more comfortable at Evangel Temple. I kept teaching my class at University Heights, and we maintained strong ties there. It was like we were "duly aligned".

Sharon can tell her own story, but in the early 70's she began to go to meetings and Bible studies with people from all different denominations. What was different about them was that they were part of a large movement throughout the country known as the "Charismatic Movement". These groups were tuned into the leading of the Holy Spirit with a strong emphasis on things such as being "filled with the Spirit", and "speaking in tongues". She was searching for some spiritual help, and meaning in her life, and thought she might find it there. I thought it was the screwiest thing I had ever heard of, and accused her of wanting to become some kind of "Holy Roller". I was troubled that she would allow herself to get involved with people who did such things.

When she came home one evening, and told me that she had received the "baptism of the Holy Spirit", and had spoken in tongues, I was shocked out of my gourd. I didn't know what to do. This whole thing had gone too far. The problem was that I could see she was a changed person. Her whole countenance was bright and shining and new. I couldn't deny that something had indeed happened to her. The best part was in her attitude toward me. She became a truly loving and wonderful wife. I'm not saying she was perfect, but for quite a while, things definitely got better for me. She was loving, understanding and forgiving. How could I object to something so positive?

Out of curiosity I began to go to some of these meetings too, only with other men. St. James Episcopal Church had a rector by the name of Doug McGlynn who was into this, and there was a small men's prayer group at his church. I saw things happening in these meetings, and to these men that I had never seen before. At first I was a little put off, and uneasy with the speaking in tongues, but I realized that they had something that I didn't, and instead of being offended by it, I gradually began to seek it. It took a long time for me, and I became quite discouraged. Then one Saturday morning at St. James, Doug and a few other men were praying with me and it happened. I spoke in tongues and immediately I felt filled with the wonderful presence of God.

Doug McGlynn and David Rees Thomas were good friends. David was pastor of Evangel Temple. That's how I met David, and why we started going to Evangel Temple. For years, Sharon and I were very much involved, and even had a prayer and Bible study group in our home. It seems that through the years that spark of deep spiritual commitment has slowly died. Not just in us, but in many that we knew through those times. You don't hear much about the Charismatic Movement anymore. It seems to be a part of history. What was it? Why did it happen to us? Why didn't it last? It was like passionate romantic love - "Too hot not to cool down". Was it just some spiritual phase we went through? Some kind of Spiritual puberty? I don't know the answer. I only know that the way I was then, and the way I am now could not be more different. It was definitely a good thing. It helped us through some rough spots. It's definitely what we needed then. Maybe we have matured spiritually.

In the summer of 1982 we discovered that my mother had terminal colon cancer. She was only 66 years old, still working, seemingly a picture of health. She left Webster and came to live with us. She had always been a strong Scientist. She now turned to God to face the most serious problem she had ever dealt with. She agreed to surgery (there was nothing they could do), and she agreed to chemo-therapy. For a person who had spent her entire adult life independent of doctors and medicine, she was a model patient. She did all those things her family wanted her to do. But her faith was not in her doctor, but in God. It appeared to me, and I believe it appeared to her, that God had let her down, had abandoned His most faithful servant in her hour of greatest need. Eventually we gave up hope that she would survive. We knew she would die.

Accepting death, which is inevitable for all of us, is one thing. Accepting horrible suffering, embarrassment and humiliation, is something else. My wonderful mother suffered terribly as the cancer ravaged her body. By the time she died there was nothing left of her. No place to inject the morphine which hardly touched the pain. She appeared to give up on God. Gave up on the Bible. She couldn't understand "why", and neither can I. She died on June 30, 1983, at the age of 67.

The death of a loved one is always hard. Grief is inevitable. But my mother's death, and particularly the way she died, caused me to question everything I believed about God. Anger toward God is not a feeling unique to me, many have experienced it, but it was my first time. Some things were no longer making sense to me. The final blow was yet to come. I continued much the same as before. I went through the grief process. Mom had gotten so bad that her death was a relief in many respects.

On March 6, 1990, my 26 year old son Tony was involved in a fatal traffic accident. He died on March 8, 1990. I have yet to recover from this, and I doubt that I ever will. It has had a profound effect on my religious views. I would have to admit that I have become very skeptical of a lot of commonly held Christian beliefs. The idea that God is love, which I easily held since a boy, no longer seems reasonable to me, to my human logic and reason. I realize that the Bible says, "God's ways are not man's ways", and that "His thoughts are not our thoughts", but still, I only have a human mind to work with. That human mind that presumably God gave to me tells me that if God were love, if He loved me and His creation, things would not be as they are. He could fix it in a nanno-second if He wanted to.

Since Tony died I have read a lot of books such as, "Why Bad Things Happen To Good People", all of which deal with the problem of just what in the world is God doing? There are no good answers, either from those who try to defend God and Christianity, or those who decide that God doesn't exist. In my own lifetime there have been events so horrible that they stagger the mind. The Holocaust, Bosnia, Oklahoma City, The Twin Towers. The list is endless. God either causes these events, allows them to happen (even though He could prevent them) or allows them to happen because He has no power to prevent them. If He causes them, then in my opinion He is not a loving God. Likewise, if he allows them and can prevent them, He doesn't love us. If He has no power or very limited power, then He could love us, but the idea of an omnipotent, all powerful God goes out the window. At least we can't be angry with Him if He's as helpless as we are.

But if He's helpless then he should set the record straight, and not keep on masquerading as all powerful etc. If He's more like the Wizard of Oz, then it's time to pull back the curtain and let us all in on the secret. Some of my friends say that it is presumptuous to question God, and the real problem is that I just don't see it as God sees it. He can see the "big picture", and I can't. They may not realize it, but what they are saying is that bad may be good. Of course if that's true, then good may be bad, and right may be wrong. If God lives in a topsy - turvy world then wouldn't it <u>all</u> be topsy - turvy to us? You can't have it both ways. Well, maybe in God's world you can. Maybe it's more like Alice In Wonderland than we know. Maybe up is down.

So what do I believe? I don't know. I don't know what to believe. Of all the competing religions and philosophies it is possible that:

(1) None are right;

(2) All are right;

(3) 1 or some are right.

Of course some religions and beliefs seem preposterous. But who is to say? If we are to leave reason and logic out of it, the man who worships his navel may be just as correct as the Pope. Some say "sincerity" is everything, and others say "you can be sincerely wrong". Isn't it amazing that with all this diversity and confusion there are so many people who steadfastly claim to have all the answers, and declare all others as hopelessly wrong.

So what do I believe? Something? Nothing? Here is what I think, but I realize full well that I could be totally wrong.

1. There must be a God or gods. There must be an intelligent Creator. I don't believe that man, and the Universe are just some cosmic accident.

2. I don't have any idea how God did it, but I do not believe in the literal account of creation in the Bible. Not in the story of Adam and Eve or the Garden of Eden. (If there was such a place we'd have found it by now)

3. I believe that the Bible contains a lot of facts and truth. If God wrote it, directed it or inspired it, then He is not a very good writer or communicator. We are definitely overdue for a sequel or a new edition to clear up all the confusion surrounding it.

4. Different people would say that God has told us all we need to know in The Bible, The Koran, the teachings of Buddha, Confucius, etc. I believe that the Creator of the Universe could surely communicate the truth to us if He wanted to. He could do it in a clear, concise manner so that there would be no doubt about what He said. Everyone would know it was from God. There would be no guesswork, no speculation, no doubts. Everybody would be on the same page.

5. God is either limited in His ability to communicate with us or chooses not to clearly communicate with us. If God would just tell me the whole Truth, so I could understand it, and then give me all power, I could get the whole world cleaned up in less than a month, and nobody would have to get hurt.

6. Why would God be so vague? I don't know. Maybe it's because He doesn't want us to know what He knows. Then we would be too much like Him. Maybe we wouldn't fear or respect Him enough. Even though we had the knowledge we wouldn't have His power unless "knowledge truly is power". Maybe He really didn't want Eve to eat from the tree of knowledge.

7. The <u>Game</u> <u>Theory</u> of <u>Life</u>. Perhaps you have never heard of this. It is a "theory" that I have developed to possibly explain the mess we are in. God could let us know the Truth, but He has chosen not to for whatever reasons He may have. Maybe He thinks it would be too boring for Him and for us. If we didn't have religion and politics then we might all get along instead of killing each other. How dull.

God doesn't keep all the Truth from us. He lets us find some, and we need this Truth to navigate through life safely. Look at it as a giant video game. If you figure it out you can go along and not get zapped. If you goof up you're history. Game over. If we want to survive for as long as possible, we've got to figure out the game. It's never boring. It may be terrifying, but never dull, for us or God. He doesn't often interfere, but sometimes he may choose to reach down and keep us or save us from disaster. That may be why He created angels. There is no logic to who He might help on a given day. For some reason He didn't help the six million or so that were killed in the Holocaust, but then there are a few survivors who believe they were spared by God's intervention. We might call this random goodness. But it can't be counted on, and it's not really goodness, because it is random and selective. It just keeps us in the game a little longer.

I am still a Christian. I realize that there is much disagreement over what that means. This may not be the kind of "faith" that God is looking for, but it seems to me that you can't go wrong being a Christian. What do you have to lose? I am no expert on other religions, but do any of them say that if you are a Christian you are doomed? I don't think so. Well, maybe Islam and a few do. Christianity makes that bold statement. That it is the "only way", not just a way. So you would be crazy not to be a believer. From what I can see, the only thing Christianity can promise us is "eternal life" with God. It won't keep me from harm, from getting sick. It won't make me rich or smart. There are a lot of poor, dumb, sick Christians. It helps give me some peace of mind about life so that I don't get totally stressed out when bad stuff happens. It helps me meet and be loved by a lot of good people. I'm not giving up. I'll keep searching. Just don't tell me any stupid stuff, and pass it off as Truth.

CHAPTER ELEVEN

•Hobbies, Travel and Interests•

I don't have any hobbies like stamp collecting. If sports can be a hobby then I have one. I love to play sports more than watch, but as you get older you watch more than you play. I wouldn't think of playing a serious game of football now, but I like to throw one around, and usually we'll have the "Family Thanksgiving Day Touch Football Game". When "March Madness" rolls around I can be just as crazy as the next guy.

I have had some interests besides sports in my life. When I was about 8 or 9 years old I took piano lessons for a couple of years. We had an old upright piano in the living room so I could practice. Of course, I always wanted to be outside playing when it was time to practice, but Mom made me stick to it. Dad was never supportive, and always complained about the expense. I guess I finally quit because Mom got tired of trying to get me to practice. I had a lesson every week, and practiced some most every day. I gave several recitals along

217/THE ACCIDENTAL LAWYER

with my teacher's other students. I remember those as terrifying experiences. It seems like all of them were at Lockwood or the Little Theater at Webster High.

Albert Smith lived next door to us on Summit, and was a few years older than me. He took no lessons, and had no piano. He would come over and "play by ear". I have no idea how that is possible, but I was always amazed. I took lessons and practiced every day, and struggled through stuff like "The Happy Train", and he just sat down and played anything he'd heard.

The piano didn't have a bench, it had a round stool. You could raise or lower it by turning the seat. I remember sitting on the stool and not playing the piano. I was just sitting there twisting back and forth, and probably mouthing a little more than I should have. Dad was sitting on the couch next to the stool, and told me to be quiet. I didn't do it or didn't do it fast enough, and the next thing I knew he was lunging at me, trying to hit me. I just spun off that seat, and out of the way, to avoid the blow. Instead of hitting me, he hit the piano, and broke his finger. I can still remember him dancing around the living room in pain and yelling, "The damn kid ducked, the damn kid ducked". Until he died at 86 I would occasionally remind him of that incident. He would always smile.

The piano was pretty much it for my musical career, except that I earlier mentioned my singing in the choir in grade school, and at

Principia. I also mentioned the normal grade school plays, and two musicals at Principia, Brigadoon and Tony Beaver. I'm sure that you are familiar with Brigadoon, but Tony Beaver? In 1954 we were the first to ever put this musical on. We may have also been the last. I don't remember much about it except the story centered around a giant water melon, and a bunch of Hillbillies. Anyway, I was in the chorus of both musicals. The only play I was in in high school was Julius Caesar by Shakespeare. I played the part of Cassius. Near the end of the play, after the forces of Mark Anthony are about to defeat the betrayers, I order my servant to kill me. We were using a real sword, and when he ran me through, he nicked my side and drew blood. I did a very convincing death scene.

At Drury I had a couple of fraternity brothers who were Drury Lane troopers, Ralph Dickinson and Rick Wuertz. They helped promote my acting career. My biggest part was as Thomas in Moliere's "The Imaginary Invalid" in 1956. Back in those days Drury theater was one of the main cultural events in Springfield. Drury also had annual "State of The Union" performances, and I had major roles in those as well.

After I started practicing in Springfield I tried out for a part in the Little Theater production of "Gypsy". It's a musical based on the life of a famous stripper named Gypsy Rose Lee. I ended up with 3 parts. I was the voice over the intercom on all the shows in the show,

Pasty, the gay stage manager, and the grumpy old owner of the theater where Gypsy performed. It called for quick costume changes, and the curtain call was real tricky. I always wanted to try out again, but I just never had the time. This was in the 60s at Central High Theater. I still love to go to the theater, and in 1993, had the chance to see some great shows on Broadway such as "Grand Hotel", "Will Rogers Follies", and "Miss Saigon". Now that there are traveling Broadway troupes that come to Springfield, and St. Louis, it is possible to see a lot of great theater without the hassle and expense of the New York scene. Even Branson has had the Rocketts Christmas Show. We've seen "Phantom of the Opera", "Les Miserables", "Oliver", "Cats", "42nd Street", and lots of others.

I can't say that travel is my favorite thing to do, but each time I have ventured forth I have enjoyed it, and fondly look back on the experience. When I was a kid growing up we didn't travel much because we didn't have any money, and people just didn't do it like they do now. The only family trips that I remember were to Lake Norfork a couple of times, and Kentucky Lake once. Of course we'd make the 50 mile trip between Washington and Webster now and then. My senior class went to Washington D.C. I was the only one not to go because I had no money. That was weird. I bet they had a good time.

Except for a little travel with the Marines to California I didn't take any trips until I was married, and had a family of my own. The first real trip was in 1967, when Mom, Sharon, Teddy, Tony and I went camping to French Lake Canada. I bought an Appleby Tent Camper for this, and off we went. Paige was just a baby, and stayed with her aunt Mary and uncle Anthony McConnell. There were a few memorable moments on that trip. On the way we stopped at a camp in Iowa. I noticed Mom sneaking of to wash her new dentures. I discovered that she had picked up Peaches' flea soap by mistake. She had no fleas in her mouth the rest of the trip.

While in Minnesota or Wisconsin I was standing with Mom at a scenic overlook site. A bronze marker explained the geology and formation of what we were looking at. It was millions of years old. Mom, who had little concept of history asked, "Was that before the time of Christ?" Once when she and I got in a discussion about her using a more modern version of the Bible than the King James version, she sternly told me "that if it was good enough for Jesus, it was good enough for her". I couldn't argue with that.

One night I heard a thud near the camper. I couldn't figure out what it was, but later discovered that Tony had fallen out of the camper onto the ground below. He was sleeping so soundly it didn't wake him. At French Lake there had been this fantastic long distance canoe race. We went down to the beach and finish area, and watched them come in. It was quite a party and a colorful sight.

Later that night we were back at our campsite around the fire when a voice called to us from the darkness of the lake, "How far to the finish line?" These guys were about 8 hours behind the rest. We all had a good laugh at their expense. We vowed we'd never camp again in Canada or the northern U.S.A. because of the mosquitoes and flies. They are vicious. They found Sharon and Tony especially tasty. Teddy was 6 and Tony was 4.

We used to camp a lot around the area lakes, but the other major trip we took was in June of 1974 or so, when we went to Colorado. We had all our family, and our niece Lisa Biesinger. Lisa was going through a sort of rebellious teenage thing, and she kept it interesting. We loved the mountains except when my LTD Ford Station Wagon wouldn't pull us and the camper up the "Million Dollar Highway" out of Ouray. We had a harrowing time stuck on the mountain, and a thrilling ride being pulled off by a wrecker. It was an exciting trip, especially when Lisa fell in love with a young hitch-hiker we encountered at a campground. Suddenly I felt very old.

Sharon and I took our first trip overseas in March of 1972, when we went to Spain. This was a Missouri Bar trip to Majorca, and we became friends with Bud Bates and his wife, and Tom Wheatley, and his wife Phyllis from Kansas City. It's a beautiful island in the Mediterranean Sea. We rented a car, and hit the back roads. It was very enlightening to get away from the tourists. We stopped at a small country Catholic Church, and had prayer. This was also my first chance to see a castle, and a moat. Always before it was in a Robin Hood movie. Everything in Europe is so old and full of history. We took a side trip to Madrid on the Mainland, and had a great tour of the Prado. What made it so good was our guide who was a history and English major, with unbounded enthusiasm for her subject. Each room in the King's palace was more unbelievable than the next. We had left our kids with a babysitter for 2 weeks. When we got home she was out in the driveway with them, and her bags packed. As soon as I paid her she was gone. I got the feeling our 3 little darlings had been quite a handful.

Our best trip was in 1984, when we went to visit Tony, who was in school at Oxford, England. We flew to New York, Amsterdam, and then Brussels, Belgium. There we stayed off and on with Cody and Sharron Pelham. He was Dean of Continental Bible College at the time. Brussels and Belgium were great places, and Cody and Sharron wonderful hosts. From there we went to Switzerland, Germany, Paris, and the Netherlands. We took the train everywhere, which in Europe is the only way to go. We had our fill of castles. The Rhine Cruise was full of them. Most of the time we had no idea where we were or what we were doing, but it all worked out swell.

Paris was an exciting place, but we only got to spend 3 days there. Tony said it was his favorite city. We took a tour of the Breendonk

Concentration Camp in Belgium. What a sobering place. I still cannot imagine the inhumanity of man towards his fellow man.

We crossed the English Channel by Hovercraft from Calais to Dover. We saw the "white cliffs". We took a bus to London, and to Oxford, which is 50 miles from London. It was late when we finally found Tony in his flat at 106 Banbury Road, Flat L. We got a room at the Galaxy Hotel down the street. I wrote a book about Tony called, "His Wonderful Life". There is more detail there about this trip. Suffice it to say that we had 5 great days at Oxford with him where I learned to punt on the Charnwallis, saw Buckingham Palace at Woodstock, played tennis on grass for the first time, hit all the neat Oxford pubs, such as Turf Tavern, Eagle & Child (C.E. Lewis' hangout), Brown's, and others, and saw Tony play in the championship basketball game for Regent's College. I was completely taken in by the intellectual and historical mystique of the place. I hope to go back someday, though I know it will be sad.

We spent our last 4 days in London with Tony. We saw all the touristy sites such as The Tower of London, Buckingham Palace, Hyde Park, St. James Park, Piccadilly Circus, Regent's Park, West Minister Abbey, Horse Guards, House of Parliament, and Covent Gardens. We saw 3 plays there, "Run For Your Wife" at the Claridon, "Evita" at Prince Edward Theater, and "Noises Off" at the Savoy Theater. At Heathrow we bid a sad farewell to Tony, and flew back to Missouri.

Except for a couple of weeks in the Bahamas in June of 1989, and Victoria, Canada in 1998, we haven't been out of the country. Trips to New York, Texas, Oregon, Washington, Virginia and Florida have been it so far.

I like to read. One of my great frustrations in life is not having the time to read, and knowing that each day more books are published than I could read in a lifetime. I'm paying now for that long dry spell in my life when I didn't read anymore than I had to. For being a lawyer, rather than an English or History teacher.

CHAPTER TWELVE

•Friends•

F riends are very important. I have had good friends. The problem is that as time goes by you lose track of old friends. They move, you move. Your circumstances change. You make new friends. I've always wondered what you do about your old friends? It is almost impossible to keep those relationships up. How hard should you try? Ma Bell wants us to try real hard.

I've mentioned my friends growing up and in high school, college and law school. It's always good to see them. It's always dangerous to mention names for fear you'll forget someone. I've had lots of friends, but some special friends who have been there for me at tough times in my life are Larry and Meredith Bass, John and Judy Martin, Ted Nickle, John, Jan and Gay Lewis, Dennis and Barb Gaylor, Cody and Sharron Pelham, Dick and Jane Dunn, John and Gloria King, Aundrae and Glenys Curtis, Cal and Kathy LeMon, Steve Fielding, Bob Kinloch, Phil and Gail Pierce, Lorne Kenyon and Jane Maddox,

Mike and Martha Brooks, Monte and Sue Doing, David and Betty Carlton, Bob and Connie White, and Shirley VanStavern. Many of those just mentioned are now deceased. Larry and Meredith Bass, John Martin, Jan Lewis are gone.

I was 60 on May 5, 1996. My friends and family knew that I absolutely did not want any celebration of this event, because I firmly believed there was nothing to celebrate. May 5th came and went, and aside from a small family dinner etc., there was no party. Weeks went by and I was convinced that what I feared was not going to happen. There would be no big surprise party. Now I was dejected because I didn't believe they would take me so literally. However, on May 25th we went to John and Judy Martin's cabin at Lindenlure on the Finley River to acknowledge Memorial Day weekend. When we got in the cabin there were 60 or so friends crammed in there yelling surprise and singing happy birthday. I was indeed surprised. The good feelings lasted for only a minute or so because suddenly and tragically the deck behind the cabin collapsed, and catered food, boiling oil and water, along with people went spilling some 15 to 20 feet to the ground. Many were hurt and burned quite severely including my wife Sharon. It was terrible, and a birthday party to remember. Ever since then, no one has ever agreed to attend a birthday party for me. Even good friends have their limits. It is just as well. I never want to stop having birthdays, but I can do without those cruel cards and gifts that remind one of the fact that you may be living on borrowed time. Geezer status is too easily attained!

I will never outgrow my need for my friends. They sustain us and give life flavor. I'm sure there will be new friends I haven't met yet. I say to one and all. Thank you.

CHAPTER THIRTEEN

•The Law•

Even though my choosing of the law as a profession was pretty much a fluke (The Accidental Lawyer), for the most part I have enjoyed it. Outside of teaching, I can't imagine what else I would have done. When I was very young, I wanted to be a fighter pilot, even though I'd never flown. I could have been a psychologist. What I really wanted to do was be a coach. But that day in the CX with Hough and McGuire headed me to law school and the law. By the way, both of them recently retired as judges.

My last semester in law school at St. Louis University I started thinking about what I should do. I could get in a military JAG corps, join the FBI, teach some place, get a job with a corporation in its law department, or actually practice. I decided to practice law, but where? I was still working part time for Judge Hensley in the Probate Court, so I asked him for advice. He said, "Ted, you'll make a good living wherever you go, so go some place you would like to raise your kids". I always assumed I would stay in St. Louis, but with crime and other problems, I decided that maybe Springfield would be a better place.

I graduated on June 4, 1990 at Keil Auditorium. I immediately started to study for the Missouri Bar Exam, which was the last 3 days of June in Jefferson City. I knew what subjects would be on the bar, and how many days I would have to review. I carefully planned what I was to study on each day. I couldn't let anything interrupt that schedule. It was a terrible 4 weeks, and I was not nice to be around. I missed a wedding and a funeral. Nobody was speaking to me. The truth is that I was scared to death I would not pass the bar. My whole future depended on it. My ego was in jeopardy.

Most of the guys were taking a bar review course downtown called Hardy's Bar Review. I wasn't because I had no money for it. One night they snuck me in because it was a subject I hadn't had or one I was a little weak in. On the way home I was going down Lindell Blvd. past the law school. A burly St. Louis cop stopped me right in front of the law school, claiming I had run a red light. I was pleading with this guy for my life because to pay for a ticket would be impossible. He was about to take pity on me and let me go. Then several law students stopped when they saw I had been pulled over. These fledgling lawyers started to give the cop a bad time and argue my case. When he found out I was a law student, and so were all these characters, he quickly wrote out the ticket and drove away. I thanked them for all their help.

Since I had no money to pay a fine with, I appeared in City Police Court to plead my case. That turned out to be a pretty sleazy place, but the judge was sympathetic, and found that I hadn't run the light. I got a speeding ticket a little later, but by the time it was set for trial, I was in Springfield. One of my law school buddies, Chuck Deba, was a City Prosecutor, and he said he'd "fix it" for me. Instead he plead me guilty, and told me to send money for the fine. I never have figured out how the prosecutor pled me guilty.

Those 3 days taking the bar were the worst ever. The test back then was all essay, so after writing all day for 3 days you can't believe the case of writer's cramp that I had. To make matters worse it was about 95 degrees and the air conditioning broke. I was sweating all over my blue books.

A lot of guys were staying at the Holiday Inn. Don Gunn and I roomed together. I had studied and reviewed. Now I knew it was time to relax, and get a good night's sleep each night. Don was going out of his mind. He couldn't sleep. He moaned, he groaned. I had my pillow over my head desperately trying to sleep. He was going to ruin me. Once I looked up and he was walking on top of the dressers moaning and crying. The second night I told him that if he did that again I'd throw him out. He did, but I was so tired I slept right through it.

After the bar exam, a bunch of us went to a local pub to discuss it. This was not good because many of the answers some of them came up with were not the ones I had. I finally could take it no more and left for Springfield. Instead of taking any break I started work the very next day. Some of those Missouri and Washington University guys who were so sure of their answers failed the bar. Everyone from St. Louis University passed the bar except one. We had one girl in our class. She was a very nice person, but she never did pass the bar. This experience colored my opinion about women lawyers for a long long time.

In March of 1960, I came to Springfield to interview with law firms for a job. It was a very exhausting process. The lawyers who conducted the interviews were very nice, and I had a positive feeling about the Springfield Bar. I was in the old Landers Building (now State Office Building) talking with a lawyer, and looking down at my car parked on the street. I got to observe a meter maid giving me a parking ticket. I stayed with Mitch and Mary Ann Hough that week. Mitch had graduated a semester early (probably by cheating), and was already working in the Prosecutor's office.

I went to Christian County with him to assist in the trial of a drunk driver. I'm not sure why the case was in that county. This was my first real trial. Of course, I didn't do anything but sit at the counsel table. The judge was a local character by the name of Herb Taylor. The judge had trouble staying awake before lunch. After lunch he had trouble doing anything. It appears that he drank his lunch somewhere, a not uncommon occurrence. The afternoon was a total fiasco, and the judge's sympathies and habits lay with the Defendant. I came away a little disillusioned.

I was offered and I accepted a job with Miller, Fairman, Sanford, Carr and Lowther. After the bar exam I drove to a new duplex we had rented at 2020 E. Page, and started work the next morning. I've been working ever since. Contrast this with my son Tony who took 2 months to study for the bar, and when it was over spent a month in Europe before he started work at Shook Hardy and Bacon in Kansas City. Tony was much smarter than his old man, but I was married to a pregnant wife and I had no choice.

At the time I started with Miller Sanford we had 10 lawyers, and were the biggest firm in town. The office was at 926 Woodruff Building. My office was not great, nor were the furnishings. Everything was old, and nothing matched. I did have a great view out my window. They started me at the outlandish sum of $350 per month. It took me about 6 years before I made as much as my Chevrolet plant guard job paid when I was in law school. This was not a program to get rich on. I knew the concept of "starving lawyers" first hand.

My great fear was that I would work there a couple of months, and then find out that I hadn't passed the bar exam. We didn't find out until September 3, 1960. My "friend" Tom McGuire couldn't wait for the official notification. He drove to Jefferson City to see the results as they were posted by the Supreme Court. He said he would call me. He called and said my name wasn't on the list. I was devastated. I couldn't believe it. I didn't tell anyone at the firm. I was too embarrassed. He let me stew all day, and then that night he called and said it was a joke. I had passed. Some joke. Lucky for him he was in Jefferson City. I was pretty steamed. The next day I got the official telegram from the Court. It said "Passed Bar Examination". What a relief.

My first day on the job was taken up with meeting everyone, and getting settled in. One of the people I met was Sam Hamra, who had started work only a few months before I did. Later in the day Sam showed up with an armload of files for me. He said these were the cases that the "new guy" always got. I didn't remember anyone telling me I was working for Sam, but I took them without saying anything. They were a bunch of dog cases that people had been working on for years. When Jim Prewitt joined the firm a few months later I took great pleasure in handing them off to him.

It's quite possible that even today some new young lawyer is still working one of those old files at Miller, Sanford.

I only lasted 7 months at Miller, Fairman. There were a lot of good people and good lawyers there, but it was my misfortune to be assigned to William P. Sanford. Bill Sanford was a very fine, and capable lawyer, but he came down on me like a ton of bricks. Not only was it his responsibility to assign work for me to do, he also was to train me to be a lawyer. God knows I needed a lot of training. After 3 years of law school I had little comprehension of what a lawyer did. I have always felt that his methods were too extreme. Instead of encouraging and nurturing he chose to browbeat and harangue me. There was absolutely nothing that I could do that was right or pleased him. All my work, from the complicated to the routine, would come back marked up by his "red pen". I laugh about that now because there have been secretaries, and young lawyers who have complained about my vicious red pen. They didn't know Bill Sanford.

The situation got so bad that I couldn't drive to the office in the morning without my stomach knotting up. I finally had to quit. Even though that 7 months was like "legal boot camp", I did do some memorable things, and learned a lot from old Bill. When you start out, there are a lot of "firsts". My first job was Miller, Fairman. My first secretary was Llenyce Meister, from Miller, Missouri. My first ulcer was Bill Sanford. My first client was ....., well I can't remember her name, but I'll never forget what happened. Lets call her Jane.

For 4 months I had just worked on cases that Sanford assigned to me. I had no clients of my own. Even though I was 24 years of age I looked 18. Sometimes clients that Sanford would bring to my office would get that look in their eye. I knew what they were thinking. "Is this guy even out of high school? He can't be a real lawyer". I know now that they had reason to be concerned. Young lawyers really don't know anything or worse, how to do anything. Then one day I got a call from Jane. I had been recommended to her by a mutual friend. She wanted a divorce. My first client. She made an appointment.

There is something exciting about your first client. I was anxious to meet her. The problem was that I didn't know anything about divorce. I hadn't taken Domestic Relations in law school. All I had been doing for the firm was research, and insurance defense work. I panicked. I wanted to do a good job. I wanted to impress Jane with my knowledge. I dashed to the law library, and started reading all I could about divorce. I talked to a few lawyers in the firm who I thought did some of it. By the time Jane showed up I was a boy expert on the subject.

Jane had a real tale of woe. She was married to a major in the Army who was head of the R.O.T.C. program at S.M.S. They had 5 boys. He was violent, and very abusive toward her. He had guns. She was afraid to leave, but had to get out. She was positive that he was having an affair. He had threatened to kill her, and her lawyer if she ever tried to leave. Just your simple divorce I thought. I had more guts than brains, so I jumped right in.

I had seen enough stuff on TV and in the movies to know that in this kind of case you had to "get the goods" on the other side. This was long before the days of "no fault" divorce. I decided that adultery would be our big weapon, but we had to have proof. I didn't know any private investigators, and even if I had, Jane couldn't have afforded one. I saw it as my duty to get the evidence we needed. This led to a couple of ridiculous situations. I told her to call me anytime she thought she had some inkling that he was running around. She did.

Teddy was born October 25, 1960. Shortly thereafter Sharon was invited to a very nice bridge party at Jean Prewitt's house. I was to baby-sit with the kid. Sharon had been gone about an hour when Jane called and told me that she was sure her husband, and the other woman, were together at a downtown bar. We finally had a chance to catch him. I called Sharon at the party, and told her I had to go out. I was bringing Teddy to the party. She has never forgiven me. We were so poor that Teddy was wearing baby girl hand me downs. I dropped him off. He immediately got hungry, and the party stopped while Sharon nursed him. She was mortified. Meanwhile I was cruising all the downtown bars in vain. I didn't get my man. By the time I got back to the Prewitts the party was about over, and Sharon was pretty steamed.

I usually tried to come home for lunch with Teddy and Sharon as often as I could. Shortly after the bridge party incident, I came down a side street about two blocks from our duplex. There were no houses there, just woods. I passed this parked car with a couple making out in it. It was my man! When I got to the house I told Sharon to bundle up Teddy in his car seat, and come with me. Meanwhile, I got our old Brownie camera. It was the kind where you had to roll the black and white film after each picture. I told Sharon about the bad guy being parked near our house in the woods. She was to drive, and I would hide in the back seat of our 1959 Nash Rambler. When we got next to his parked car she was to stop, and I would pop up and take a picture. She was scared to death. I admit that my heart was beating pretty fast. Only Teddy was calm. It worked perfectly. When we got alongside, he came out of his clinch to see what was going on. I sprang up and took his picture. He tried to get out of his car. I told Sharon to pull up so I could get a picture of the back of his car, and his license plate.

Meanwhile I'm trying to roll the film. I got a good shot, and told her to "step on it".

For some reason it never occurred to me that he would not take this lying down. Suddenly I realized he was turning his car around and coming after us. What followed was a very wild car chase through the City of Springfield for about a half hour. Sharon was screaming and crying. I was yelling driving instructions to her from the back seat, and Teddy joined in and began to cry and scream. We were all pretty hysterical. I remembered the guns and the death threats. At that point I was pretty convinced that I had made a major mistake. We broke all the speed limits, and ran a lot of red lights, but we finally lost him.

For weeks after that I expected to be ambushed by this guy. Wouldn't you know that the Army transferred him, and old Jane went along. I don't know if they ever got a divorce, but that case took several years off my life. I did learn that it wasn't my job to be a hero, and I let somebody else get the evidence after that.

Another good thing that came from my time at Miller Fairman was my friendship with Jim Prewitt. We discovered our mutual love of basketball and sports in general, so we joined the YMCA a few blocks from the office. For many years he and I would play basketball on our lunch hour. We started the "Lawyers Basketball Team" in 1960 or 1961, and played together for many years on that team with guys like John Lewis, Hank Westbrooke, Jerry Lowther, Duane Cox, Thom Field, Kerry Montgomery, Dick Wilson, and many others.

Jim and I shared a locker at the Y. I guess it was cheaper. You get to know a guy pretty well when you share a locker. I took my stuff home to be washed pretty regularly. Jim's only flaw was that he didn't. When I couldn't stand it anymore I'd take his jock strap et. al. home for Sharon to wash. She was not particularly thrilled. Eventually Jean found out that another woman was washing her husband's jock strap, so she let Prew know that he better start bringing it home. He did. Jim and I also joined Twin Oaks together, and played some golf there. We also formed the lawyer's softball team. Besides being a good athlete, he had a fine legal mind, and we could actually discuss a little law during our one on one games.

One day Sanford asked me to go to lunch with him. Lunchtime was usually my time to escape from him. Of course I went. We were uncomfortable standing in the hall waiting for an elevator. I didn't say anything because I knew it would be wrong whatever it was. It was very awkward. Duane Cox was about 6'6" tall, and had a small office on our floor. Duane was only a year or two years older than me, and had become a notorious "ambulance chaser". He filed lots of Plaintiff's suits for "alleged personal injury", and our firm defended a lot of them. Sanford did not like him, and apparently the feeling was mutual.

Wouldn't you know that as we were standing there, Duane came around the corner to wait for the elevator too. He and I exchanged greetings. Sanford said nothing. I figured I'd be in trouble for having been friendly to Duane. Now it was really awkward. Where the hell was the elevator? Finally it got there, and as we all got in, Duane pulled out a cigar that was at least a foot long. He lit it up, took a big drag, and as he blew out a giant puff of smoke in old Bill's face said, "How ya doin Smiley?" "Smiley" Sanford was apparently Duane's pet name for Bill. Sanford turned about 8 shades of red, coughed and sputtered, and said "Just fine". I was trying very hard not to laugh. That would have been the end of me for sure. Finally we got to the lobby and headed for lunch. Duane gave me a knowing wink as we walked away. I nodded in approval. I don't believe I got chewed out anymore that day.

I had to get out of there, but where? I decided to apply for a commission with the Air Force as a JAG officer. The recruiter was very excited because I had my experience in the Marines, so I was a potential career officer. The Air Force seemed to really want me, but they couldn't get their act together. I told them I had to know by January 1, 1961, because I had another job offer, and I would take that if I didn't hear on time. They kept close contact with me, and kept assuring me everything was "go". Before Christmas I was guaranteed it would be any day. New Years came and went, and no word so I took a job with Lincoln, Haseltine, Keet, Forehand and Springer. Shortly after that the Air Force called and said my commission had come through, and my orders were being cut. I said "no way". I had already taken another job. Apparently a Colonel at some airbase in Illinois decided to go on Christmas vacation before completing my commission paperwork. I got all kinds of apologies, and his butt got chewed, but I didn't change my mind. It's not every day that the Air Force has a chance to get someone of my caliber. They blew it!

I started sometime in late January of 1961, at Lincoln, Haseltine. I stayed there until March of 1966. It only took me a few days to realize that I had made a good decision. Instead of hating to come to the office I loved it. The atmosphere was loving and nurturing, and in a short time I felt like one of the family. There were 4 partners and one associate, me. Everybody was my boss, but I primarily worked with Wally Springer and Jim Keet. After the oppressive manner of Bill Sanford, the casual and supportive approach of Wally and Jim was like a breath of fresh air. My digs improved considerably too because I inherited Harold Lincoln's office, and almost new furniture. He had been the senior partner, and had died shortly before I came on board.

To this point I have been pretty hard on Bill Sanford. I should say that after I tendered my resignation at Miller Fairman the last few weeks there weren't bad. He lightened up, and we actually got along pretty well. If he had taken that approach from the beginning I might never have left. In the following years my relationship with him was quite good. In 1967, we moved a few doors from his mother, and I was quite fond of her. In fact, our subdivision was called "Sanford Place", one of the oldies. In 1993, after he retired, I talked with him about those early days, and how hard he had been on me. I told him that even though it was very painful at the time, I had learned a lot, and it had made me a better lawyer. Sometimes there are silver linings to dark clouds.

The Lincoln firm represented about 10 insurance companies, and so I did a lot of accident investigation and defense work. I was also starting to slowly build up my own practice. I assisted in the trials of a lot of cases. Wally was better about turning me loose than Jim. I'll never forget the first time that Jim agreed to let me defend a jury trial in an auto accident case by myself. The case involved an intersection collision at Chestnut and Jefferson. Knowing his hovering ways, I made him promise that he wouldn't even come to the courthouse. He assured me that he would stay in the office.

The trial was going fine, and as I was cross examining a witness, I happened to look over my shoulder at the courtroom door. I could see Jim peering through the glass. Soon I noticed that he was in the courtroom sitting with the spectators. I was in the witnesses' face, and when I turned to go back to the counsel table, there he sat with a stupid look. By now I was pretty upset. I leaned over and said; "What are you doing here?" He said "Did you ask him about the turn signal?" I repeated, "What are you doing here?" Of course the judge, jury and whole world were watching this, and wondering what was going on. He said "I just thought you might want a little help." I laid it all on the line when I said, "Jim, either you leave or I will. You promised me you wouldn't be here. What's it going to be?" He was like a parent who couldn't let go of his child. Who couldn't accept that I was growing up. He wanted to stay in control. He made the right choice. He left. The jury returned a verdict for our side. We were both relieved that I had won. I grew 10 feet that day.

One of the big downtown furriers had been burglarized, and the police had a couple of guys from Chicago in jail for it. Horace Haseltine called me into his office and introduced me to a couple of "gentlemen" who never sat down. They were from Chicago, and looked it. They wanted to hire us to defend their buddies in jail. I could see that Horace was starting to sweat, and I didn't think he really wanted to get involved. I was sure that I didn't. So Horace said he'd take the case, but he needed a $5,000.00 retainer. This was a lot of money in those days. Of course he assumed that would run them off. Instead, one of these guys proceeded to peel off $100 bills on Horace's desk. We both looked at this pile of cash in amazement.

Horace had a big old safe in his office. The other Chicagoan said, "Where are you going to keep that money?" Horace looked at the safe and said, "In there". With an icy sneer, and a crack of his knuckles, the gentlemen exclaimed that he "could crack that in about 30 seconds". We knew we were in trouble. Horace didn't get them off, and neither of us ended up in the river.

Consumers Markets was a big grocery chain, and was insured by Liberty Mutual who we represented. I was always investigating and handling claims against Consumers. A lady slipped and fell on a grape in one of their stores, and very seriously broke her back. She was badly hurt, and had tremendous medical bills. Hal Fisher represented her in the lawsuit against Consumers. The case didn't get settled, and was going to trial. It was the first case against Consumers to actually go to trial. I had done most of the work, but Wally and I tried it together. He was there, but he graciously let me do most of it, including the opening and closing statements to the jury. Consumers and Liberty made a big deal out of it, and there along with Clarence Wheeler the President, sat all of the corporate officers. Liberty even sent their head claims man to the trial to observe. The pressure to do well, and to win, was intense. We got a defendant's verdict, and all went away happy. Except the Plaintiff.

In those days I was still young, and in pretty good shape. I sort of became Jim's body guard. One day he and I were going to lunch at Heers when a man approached Jim in a threatening manner. Jim had represented his wife in a bitter divorce. The guy lunged at Jim, but I grabbed him and knocked him up against the outside of the Holland Building. I held him there until he cooled down. Then we went on to lunch. Jim was grateful. Thereafter, when Jim was afraid things might get out of hand, he always had me around. I sat in on several depositions where things got hot, and one time had to restrain another guy who wanted a piece of Jim right there in the library. My Marine and football training were paying off.

Wally Springer was very active in a lot of civic affairs, and wanted me to be too. One of his pet organizations was the Jaycees. In deference to his wishes I joined up. Lawyers may say they are civic minded, but the primary reason they belong to all that stuff is to meet people who may become clients. Of course that's the reason most everybody joins, from insurance salesmen to real estate agents. These days they have a word for it, "networking". You can even see people do it with their church affiliations. It's shameless sometimes.

In a way I kind of enjoyed the Jaycees, at least the softball team, and the parties. We did do some good too. I was a pretty marginal member when it came to the hard work. I was there when we put on the Miss Springfield contest, and I always ran the Jaycee tennis tournament. John Crow joined the firm in 1962, and Wally suggested that I should get him involved in Jaycees too. John was probably worse than I was about joining, but I got him to go to the monthly dinner meeting with me one night. We always met in the back room of the Platter Restaurant at the corner of Glenstone and Division.

The procedure was that we would have a "Happy Hour", then we would eat, and then have a business meeting. For some reason the Happy Hour went on longer than usual, and everybody got, well, happy! Finally they brought out these big baskets of hard rolls and butter. I don't know how it started, but someone threw a roll, and before you knew it these young business and professional men were in the midst of the most wicked food fight you ever saw. I realized that I couldn't find John, and I was concerned for the safety of my guest. Each of the tables was covered with near floor length table clothes. I had seen John's bald head get hammered with a hard roll. Finally I found him cowering under a table, safely out of the line of fire. For some reason John never went back, and he never joined the Jaycees.

Like Jim Prewitt, John and his wife Janet, became good friends of ours. It was a pleasure to practice law with John. We played golf together almost every weekend for quite a while. He became a Circuit Judge, and then an Appellate Judge as did Prewitt. For some reason, the friendship you make with other lawyers at a time when you are both struggling and starting to raise your families are always special. In our case we were all products of the 40s, 50s and 60s, and those were just special times.

There are lots of other stories from those Lincoln Haseltine days, but space and time permit no more. A lot of it was just every day hard work. Ed Forehand was one of the nicest guys you would ever meet. Everyone loved Ed, and he knew every bar maid and waitress in town. He and Horace are both gone, much too early. Jim retired as a circuit judge. Wally refused to retire. He was my mentor in many ways, and I feel very fondly toward him. I regret that they told me I would have to choose between the firm and running for office. I chose politics, but there was no joy in leaving. They are all gone now, wherever lawyers go to make that final appeal.

I didn't go far from 405 Woodruff Building. Lindell Church and I shared offices on the 5th floor for a while, but that didn't work out too well, and I left and opened an office on the 10th floor near the Court of Appeals. Jim Sivils and I shared offices until Wayne Walker and I got together. Later we brought Sivils in, and called it Walker, Salveter and Sivils. Bill Wendt and Keith Williams rented space from us there on the 10th floor. At some point Sivils left, and it was Walker and Salveter for quite a while. When the Court of Appeals wanted to expand they took our space and we moved our offices to 318 Woodruff Building. It was there that I hired Bill Stoner to work for me. In 1976, he and I bought the old Lawson Gibbs Title Company building at 915 Boonville, across from the courthouse. We completely gutted it, added to it, and ended up with a building that would house 6 lawyers. Bill was made a partner and we called it Walker, Salveter & Stoner.

Stoner and I were both fitness nuts, so on the first floor we had an exercise room with a shower and sauna. Ed Lee clerked for me in the summers when he was in law school at Missouri. When he got out in 1976, I hired him. Kay Graff had been our neighbor along with her husband Curtis, when we lived at 1837 S. Hampton. She decided to go to law school late in life and around 1980, when she graduated from law school at Missouri, I hired her to work for me.

When Bill and I were demolishing parts of the old building, and rebuilding, we had several interesting experiences. There used to be solid concrete steps going from the first to the second floor, and we had a guy there to jackhammer them out. He called us, and excitedly said that his jackhammer had disappeared into what appeared to be a basement. We rushed right over, because no one knew the old building had a basement. We both wondered what we would find. I imagined buried bodies or hopefully buried treasure.

249/THE ACCIDENTAL LAWYER

We shined a light down into the hole, but it was so dark we could see nothing. We put a ladder down, and Bill and I cautiously made our way to the lower recesses. The floor was grime and mud. the walls were so black that they wouldn't reflect the light. We carefully explored and found nothing. Then suddenly the light revealed an object in the corner. A coffin? A treasure chest? No, what it was, was the boiler of a very old furnace. When we touched it it disintegrated.

The builder said we should fill the basement in, but fortunately we decided to keep it. We cleaned out the gunk, poured a concrete floor, put in metal support beams, heat and air conditioning, and made it a file storage room.

Clyde Dennis had his old dingy law office up above the old abstract company. The back half of the upstairs looked like it had been a small apartment or maybe a "house of ill repute". It was all a mess. Years before, I had remembered going to Clyde's office to take a statement from him about a will he had prepared. It was creepy just to walk up those old narrow concrete steps. Clyde had a collection of antique guns up there. He also had an ominous looking moose head on the wall. His favorite thing was his arrowhead collection. He had lots of stuff. In fact there was so much stuff, it was difficult to see how he could ever find anything or get anything done. The place had a history.

When we redid the building I decided that I wanted my office to be upstairs where Clyde's was, but with a nice bay window overlooking the Greene County Courthouse across the street. I was always amused through the day by the comings and goings at the courthouse. One of my favorite things was to observe the people who would line up on Fridays to get married before Probate Judge Don Burrell, Sr. His office was on the ground floor. Even though it was a short civil ceremony, a lot of them would be decked out in formal attire and wedding gowns. Most of them looked like they had never worn a suit before, but there they were. When they grinned, a lot of them didn't have all their teeth. I usually doubted that many of those marriages would last the weekend.

For a long time we had six lawyers in the building, Wayne, me, Bill, Ed, Kay and John Kelly. John went to work for the City of Springfield. I took his office, and made it into what became known as the "Collection Department". My collection business had expanded rapidly since I represented Cox Hospital, St. Johns, Sears and a host of finance companies such as SIC, Crown Finance, Tri Continental Leasing, about 8 or 9 at one time. I also represented just about every credit union in town. To do all this required a lot of people, and it gave me opportunities to hire lots of family and friends. People that worked in collections for me were Anita Nunn, Nancy Copeland, Pat Lehman, Lara Salveter, Amy Salveter,

Meredith Bass, Pam Nickle, Patty Hartsell, Roxanne Schmidley, Lucinda Rose, and a host of others whose names do not come readily to mind. Teddy, Tony and Paige all worked in the office from time to time, especially in the summers.

Eventually Wayne retired, and died in July of 1990. Bill got into some problems trying to be a real estate developer, and left February 1, 1982. It got down to me, Ed and Kay. When Bill left I bought out his interest in the building, then around 1984, I sold the building to Jack Hogan, and leased it back. In 1994, Hogan Title took over the first floor, and we moved what was left to the second floor. In March of 1994, I decided to give up all my collection practice. I had slowly been getting rid of some of it before that. By doing this I didn't need so many people, and was in reality easing toward semi-retirement. After Tony was killed in 1990, I never seemed to have the energy or the fire to keep up with the demands of a busy practice.

Back in the 60s, when I was with the Lincoln firm, there were no public defenders, and all lawyers got appointed to defend indigent criminals for free. One day I got appointed to defend a guy named Coy Hammers on a burglary and stealing charge. The problem was that he had burgled one of the Cooper family homes, and had a gun with him when he did it. The Coopers, being a very wealthy and influential family in town, were putting a lot of heat on the Prosecutor, and the judge to throw the book at him.

Although Coy was guilty, he was taking the fall for his brother and another guy. He had no prior record, and I don't think he had the gun. I was sure that he would not have used it. He just made a dumb mistake when he had had a little too much to drink. We had no defense, and the prosecutor wouldn't plea bargain.

One day when I was visiting Coy in jail he was telling me about himself, and it turned out that he had been in the air force in Korea. It also turns out that one of our fighter planes landed and was on fire. Coy was not a pilot. He rushed out to the plane, and pulled the pilot from the flaming cockpit. He saved the guy's life. Well it turns out that this wasn't just any guy, but was Ted Williams, the famous baseball player. It dawned on me that a guy who had been a war hero, and who had saved the life of one of the greatest hitters of all time, should get a shot at probation.

At the time Williams was a spokesperson for Sears, and I was finally able to locate him. He verified the story, and said he would do what he could to help. Then I started to try my case in the press and of course it made quite a story. None of it much impressed the Coopers. They wanted his scalp. We had this big hearing where I was trying to convince the judge to grant probation. The thing got so serious that both Judge Collinson and Judge Green heard it.

I had learned from a reliable source that the Coopers were putting direct political pressure on Judge Green. I also heard that his sympathies were with my war hero, but he knew what was good for his political future too. The Sheriff was Glen Hendrix, and he got in the act. Everybody seemed to be against my guy. The hearing was not going well. I was a little immature and overzealous. I panicked and dropped the bomb that the judges were being swayed by outside forces. Collinson was upset and swore no one had tried to influence him. Green stood up and he and I had quite a heated exchange. The reporters loved it. I calmed down when they threatened to throw me in jail for contempt of court.

I wish I knew where my old file on that and other cases was. Poor old Coy got sent to prison. He took it all in stride. I learned a lot about how local politics works. The Coopers had more votes than me and Ted Williams in Greene County. I don't believe that anyone was trying to be sinister in this. They felt seriously violated and wanted to see justice done. Coy and I were looking for a little mercy.

Back in the "good old days" Springfield had some people who were true characters. A lot of them were either suing or being sued. One of them was Joe Ray who was a friend and client for a number of years. Joe was a big brash man who claimed that he could not read or write. He lived by his wits, and did his business on a cash basis. He was involved in demolition of buildings, paving, and a host of related businesses. I first met Joe in the 60s when I hadn't been practicing very long. He came to me for a divorce. He was wearing bib overalls. I don't remember ever seeing him in anything else.

I did several divorces for him. He was not too complimentary toward women. His philosophy was it was cheaper to marry and divorce than to hire a cook, maid and prostitute. When we walked out of the courthouse after his last divorce he opined that he had been married about 20 times. He trusted me completely, and I never took advantage of him. I got him out of a lot of problems where his failure to keep records or receipts got him in trouble. He finally married Juanita, and they were together for a long time before he died.

Paul Johnson was a friend of Arl Poindexter, a good client of mine. Both were involved in a lot of litigation, and sometimes with each other. I probably had more experience suing Paul Johnson or defending suits that he filed, than anyone else. I believe that somehow litigation and turmoil gave him some sort of a rush. He had a great deal of imagination when it came to legal theories. I am happy to say that I never lost a case to Johnson. Taking his deposition or cross examining him on the witness stand was always a memorable experience. You could not waiver or be deterred by the slippery answers you would get. One of his standard answers was "I don't know, I'll have to check the records". The "records" were always hard to identify, and harder still to lay hold of. Sometimes I would notice that evidence that was used in one case would be recycled in another. Sometimes in an altered form. There was no document or record that Paul couldn't produce if given enough time. He had more corporations than the New York Stock Exchange. It was magic.

These cases covered a span of 34 years, and when I completed the last one in 1995 there was a feeling of relief, but of sadness too. An era had ended. Had we all grown too old and tired to fight, or had Paul finally run out of schemes? They don't make them like that anymore.

I remember a lady showed up at my office at 8 a.m. one Monday morning. She wanted a divorce. I was shocked to learn that she had only gotten married on Saturday. Apparently she had gone to a bar on Friday night, and got to drinking and dancing with some cowboy. It was all so good they drove over to Miami, Oklahoma and got married as soon as the wedding place opened Saturday morning. The party continued over the weekend, but by Sunday night when she sobered up, she decided it definitely was not a "marriage made in Heaven", and she was ready to call it quits. They didn't even stay together for the sake of the children!

There used to be a big pickle works at Marionville, Missouri. While unloading a big pickle vat off a truck something went wrong, and the vat rolled off, and seriously injured the driver of the truck. Everybody got sued, from the pickle factory to the trucking company. The strangest deposition I ever took was in this case. We represented one of the Defendants. There was a crucial witness who had moved back to the Arkansas hills. All the lawyers agreed to depose him at a lawyers office in a very remote Arkansas town. We all drove down, but the witness didn't show up. We all got in the local lawyers Volkswagen bus, and started to look for him. Finally we found him fishing down by the river. We had the court reporter with us, so the 5 lawyers, and the court reporter took this guy's deposition in the VW bus on the bank of the river. It was all very surreal.

In the 60s and 70s I became interested in environmental law, especially as it applied to the Ozarks. I formed a not for profit corporation with several doctors and lawyers called "The Defenders of the Ozarks Environment" DOE. The lawyers were myself, Maynard Cohick, and Larry Askinosi. The doctors were Paul Redfern PhD, Tom Tombridge, Paul Quinn and Chris Palcheff (our children's' pediatrician)

There were two issues that are worthy of note. City Utilities realized that with the rapid growth of Springfield, sufficient water would become an issue. They hired Burns and McDonald Engineers to do some studies for them. The recommendation that Burns made was that City Utilities should build a dam on or near the boundary of Greene and Webster Counties, and dam up the James river for The County Line Lake. This appeared to me to be a sweetheart deal with some influential people around here who owned a lot of the land that would be taken for the lake. We challenged this project which we felt would not meet environmental law requirements, and required that City Utilities begin crossing all the ts. They never could get an environmental impact statement to pass muster even though the Corps of Engineers seemed to be in bed with them. We suggested that the James River would be ruined, and a lot of valuable farm land along with it. Our alternative plan was to run a pipe from Stockton Lake to Springfield, and draw on that water. There were a lot of heated meetings, bad feelings, charges and countercharges. The pro growth folks were not happy, but we stopped the dam. After saying it couldn't be done, eventually they did what we suggested, and today Stockton Lake furnishes a lot of water to Springfield. I made a lot of new friends and a lot of new enemies on that deal.

DOE wasn't so much involved in the next incident. I was sort of on a lark of my own. Springfield, like all towns, is always looking to promote growth, and get new industry here. The Chamber of Commerce announced that French's Mustard was coming to town. I felt that we needed to slow growth down a bit, and that not enough thought had been given to the environmental impact on the city. French was a good solid company, and had many plants spread around the country. They were a British company, and very sensitive to their image. I went public by making a few speeches opposing the plant because of the stress it would place on water and sewer needs. There was an awful lot of by product that would be dumped into our lakes, rivers and streams via the sewer etc. The Chamber went ballistic, and French got spooked. I knew that the Chamber wasn't leveling with the public about all of this, and eventually had a mole who confided to me that all was not on the up and up. One day I secretly taped one of our phone conversations just to protect myself when I went public, and this guy wouldn't back me up. Things got real hot in the old town, and the news media loved it.

Then the strangest thing happened. The people at French contacted me and said they wanted to assure me that the plant would be a good citizen. They were going to fly me to one of their California plants and show me around. All expenses paid. I said OK if they would take the news media too. So myself, people from the Chamber, news people and others went to sunny Cal on French's dime. They wined and dined us starting on the plane with an open bar. I read "Future Shock" on the plane trip out, while most of the news boys etc. got to feeling pretty good. That was quite a trip and I became even more infamous. The plant got built, and things calmed down. Several months later, one of the TV anchors called me at the office and wanted to know if I had anything going on. I said not particularly. He said, that he had talked with a lot of the others, and they sure wished I would stir something up so they could get to go fly somewhere again. It was fun, but it takes a lot out of you to fight the whole town.

I've done about everything there is to do as a lawyer, except tax and labor law. I believe that I've done a pretty good job at all of it. There are hundreds of more law stories, but the reader has suffered enough. I've won a lot more than I've lost. In fact I really haven't lost many cases. I guess I just had good clients or was lucky. The longest case I had was the Prime, Inc. bankruptcy. It was a Chapter 11 where I represented Mercedes Benz Credit Corporation, the largest creditor. I spent a lot of time in Kansas City, St. Louis, and Springfield in the 8 years that litigation lasted. I put the kids through college on that one.

I retired from active practice on October 1, 1997. I still have my license to practice. I'm not particularly proud of the legal profession these days. The "OJ" case, crass lawyer advertising, needless litigation, excessive jury awards, and too many lawyers chasing a fast buck, make lawyers less than good role models. Maybe I'm just old fashioned. I'm happy that I can look back with pride at what I have done, and how it was in the good old days!

Bill Fulmer, industrial engineer for the company, directs Springfieldian Ed Kelly (whose duties as Chamber of Commerce representative included toting some equipment for visiting newsmen) between two production lines, while James Bovard, Fresno plant manager, accompanies attorney Ted Salveter. That's mustard (naturally) coming down the line at right. The empty cartons in the background contained empty jars, and will be reused for filled ones.

Ted in Fresno, Califomia-1972 at French Mustard Plant.

Ted teaching law and government at

Missouri State U.

CHAPTER FOURTEEN
•Summers And Jobs•

Life seems to be a blur. Everybody these days talks about how life is speeding up. The older I get the faster time flies. Rationally I know that there are still 24 hours in the day but it doesn't seem like it. Why is the pace of life picking up? Why can't we make it slow down or stop? "Stop the merry-go-round, I want to get off." I can slow things down a bit by thinking back to more sensible times and particularly those "hazy, lazy, crazy days of summer." In essence, the "good old days".

Nothing epitomizes the spirit of the old days more than my remembrances of summers in St. Louis. It still gets hot in St. Louis and because of the Mississippi, Missouri and Meremac Rivers it's always very humid. There's nothing like heat and humidity to slow things down. When we finally established roots and settled down in Webster Groves in 1944 at 548 Summit, patterns of life emerged that I could count on. One of the focal points of my summers was the big screened in porch that ran across the front and down one half the side of that dear old white stucco house.

We would sit and play out there in the cool of the morning and the warmth of the evening. Sometimes we would sleep out there and wake up to the sounds of the birds and the light of a new day. Mom made something that at the time I thought was the most wonderful stuff a person could have. All it was was Kool-Aid poured into ice cube trays. We called them "frozen suckers". Nothing was more refreshing or tasted better than a grape or orange frozen sucker on a hot evening sitting on that porch. I still looked forward to them after I was grown and gone. It took less to make us happy then. Maybe less would make us happier now.

My neighborhood gang was an integral part of my life 12 months out of the year, but especially in the summers. We set the agenda. There were no little leagues, car pools or other distractions back then. We planned the day. The only direction from our moms was to "get out of the house and play". Play we did. Baseball, Indian Ball, Fuzz Ball. We played and played. We made forts and tree houses, played cowboys and Indians, had sword fights with swords and shields we made ourselves and generally had a great time. We played cards and even a little strip poker in Billy Foster's tree house. [Every now and then girls were allowed.]

We used to wrestle and fight a lot. Usually this was controlled and friendly but occasionally it would get out of hand and someone would lose his temper. It was a great way to grow up. When it got dark we played "kick the can" and would catch lightning bugs in jars. We could sit around and talk for hours, sharing the secrets of the world with each other. One summer we discovered an old illustrated medical book in the Smith's attic. Their grandfather had been a doctor. The pictures were forbidden fruit but contributed to our general knowledge of male and female anatomy. We got caught by Mrs. Smith and the book disappeared. No matter. We were ready to move on to more revealing stuff.

B. WASHINGTON, MISSOURI

We were too poor to take many family vacations in the summer but we would go to Washington, Missouri and stay with Grandpa and Grandma Oberhaus. A lot of the time dad didn't go with us. Since mom didn't drive, and we didn't always have a car, we would catch the train in Webster and take it to Washington. Not something kids get to do anymore, unless they catch up with Amtrak somewhere. That's how people got around in those days.

Washington had a big city park and a pool. We would go there for picnics or the Friday night "fish fry" that so many small towns had back then. There was always bingo and other games going on and usually a softball or baseball game against some other town.

I went to a lot of movies as a kid. It was a major form of family entertainment before the advent of TV. I remember seeing a particularly scary movie in Washington called "The Cat People". That walk back to grandma's in the dark was one of my major being scared times. Today we wouldn't think of allowing a small boy to be out like that.

Grandpa Oberhaus (Henry) loved to take me to the "Blue Goose" for orange soda and cheese and crackers. In the evenings they loved to take me to "Lotto's", a German tavern that had the best roast beef sandwiches and beer. I didn't get the beer, just another orange soda. Grandpa told me that it kept my hair red. I loved orange soda but I didn't particularly like the red hair. That came from Mom's family. She had red hair and my uncle Raymond was called "Red". My brother Charles has it too. Dad's hair was black.

C. WATERLOO COUNTRY CLUB

Our family used to go over to George and Mildred Schuette's cabin in Illinois at the Waterloo Country Club. Dave and Don Schuette were about the same age as Charles and me. They had a big lake (no pool) with a roped off area for swimming and a giant platform and slide out in the middle. The slide was a long and fast ride down to the water. Not for the faint of heart. Many a kid bravely climbed that ladder up to the top of the slide only to chicken out and meekly climb back down. I never did, and if I did I wouldn't admit it. There were different levels of diving boards and platforms to dive off of too. It was a fun place to play.

My brother Charles is 5 years younger than me and it seems like for many of our growing up years he always wanted to follow his big brother around. Kind of like your dog that follows you out of the yard and keeps a safe distance behind. You always have to turn around, point toward home and say, "Home, go home sport"!! It hardly ever worked with the dog and it didn't work much with Charles either. "Now Charles Robert, just turn around and go back home. You can't go where I'm going. No little kids allowed! Don't make me come back there. Go!" I never had a big brother so I don't know what that rejection must have felt like for the dog or Charles. As much as I loved him, at times he could be a nuisance.

One hot summer day I was out on that platform with the big guys, sliding, diving and jumping into that deep lake water. Charles and Don were safely playing in the shallow roped off area. All of a sudden I saw Charlie leave the ropes and start to swim out where I was. I shouted at him to go back but he didn't. No matter how loud I yelled he wouldn't be deterred. Then he started to flounder and sputter and sink. I have never felt such panic as I felt then. I dove into the water and swam toward him ten times faster than I ever swam before. He was under the water by the time I got there.

Some days that lake was very clear and some days the water was murky. Fortunately, the water was clear that day and when I dove down I found him pretty quick. I got him to the top and by then there were others there who helped me get him back to shore. He coughed up half the lake but other than being scared he was okay. I was mad as hell at him and I'm sure that everyone else was too.

I can appreciate now more than then the possible tragic consequences that were avoided. Charles is 65 now, and I can't imagine what the last 60 years or so would have been like without him. He and I are the only ones left who can remember those special times of our youth, and how we fit into the bigger life around us. I loved him very much then and still do now. He doesn't follow me around much anymore, and it's been a long time since I had to tell him to go home. Someday I'll go to another place and he can't follow me there either. At least not right away. But when I see him coming then I won't tell him to go home.

D. LAKE NORFORK - BLUE WATERS RESORT

We did have one real family vacation that I remember and this involved the Schuettes too. In 1948 or 1949 we drove down to Lake Norfolk in Arkansas and stayed at the Blue Waters Resort on the Henderson side. I believe that I just finished the 7th grade. Blue Waters was owned by Wilbur and Dorothy McAfee. They liked Dave and me so much that they invited us to stay after our families went home. We did, and I went back almost every summer thereafter, and worked for Mac to earn my keep. Dave didn't go every year. The last summer I went there, was between my junior and senior year in high school.

I wouldn't spend the whole summer there. Just the last few weeks before school, and after I had earned $600 on my summer job. Back then, if you earned over $600, your parents would lose you as a deduction for tax purposes. We would help clean the cabins and do whatever odd jobs Mac wanted done. As we got older he gave us more responsibility. I became very fond of Mac and Dorothy and I think because they had no children of their own they became very fond of me too.

The summer I was 14, before my Freshman year, Mac taught me how to drive his old Chevrolet pickup truck. I drove it around the resort and occasionally out on the gravel roads around the lake. Then one day Mac did the strangest thing. He told me that there were supplies and other items that needed to be picked up in Little Rock, and he wanted me to take the truck there early the next morning. Little Rock was over 100 miles away and the highways there weren't great. I was in shock. I loved to drive that old truck more than anything, but I was only 14, and had never driven on a paved road, much less a highway.

This was my coming of age for sure. In Missouri you had to

be 16 and have a license to drive. Apparently things were looser in Arkansas. I admit that inside I was scared to death, but I told Mac I would do it. He pulled out an old Arkansas highway map (this was 1950) and showed me how to get to Little Rock, and how to get to the stores once I got there.

Dorothy fixed me a big breakfast, packed me a lunch, and off I went on a great adventure. I don't really think that Dorothy was in favor of it at all, and my parents would have been horror struck if they knew I was doing it. At this time I can't imagine it myself.

I didn't think I would ever get there, and I must have checked that map a thousand times to make sure I was on the right road. It was a hot day, and the air whipped around that cab. I drank my mason jar full of water pretty quick. I got there before noon and got the truck loaded from Mac's list at each place. It was a full load, and I dreaded a flat or blowout. I'm surprised that some Arkansas bushwhackers didn't take the whole thing from me.

I found some shade to park the truck in, bought myself an RC Cola and ate my lunch before I headed back. I have to tell you that I was pretty proud of myself on the way back, and I know I sat a little taller behind the wheel of that old truck. With that load it was slow going on the way back, but I made it home before dark. Dorothy seemed real glad to see me. Mac was proud of me, and I was proud of myself. Not your typical 14 year old's day.

1953 was my last time there. I was 17 and about to finish high school. I thought I was pretty tough, and pretty grown up. I "fell in love" that summer with Bonnie Gillette, a local girl. There were lots of girls that summer, and Mac had a brand new blue Chevrolet pickup that I loved to drive them around in. There were lots of other resorts around there, and lots of girls my age on family vacation. I made friends with Butch Blades, a local kid. Butch was a good looking guy and had his own jeep. He was well aware of all the girls that invaded his home area every summer.

Butch and I discovered about ten girls who were all there from Blythville, Arkansas. One night the two of us dated them all. We filled the truck with hay, and took them on a hayride. We took turns driving with two girls in the cab with the driver, and the rest in the back with the other. The whole thing sounded better than it actually was. It's hard to make out with lots of girls at once. Oh, Butch and I were all for it, but it didn't seem to be what the girls had in mind. There was some kissing and hand holding but not much else. We learned our lesson and just got dates with one each the next night.

Butch borrowed his dad's car and that worked out much better. One night I had the truck, and a bunch of us went to a remote spot on the lake for a midnight swim. It was dark and you could hardly see anything. We had a couple of inner tubes to hang on to out there.

That worked out pretty well too, except when we left I almost got the truck stuck and burned a goodly amount of rubber off of Mac's tires.

Butch was a classmate of Bonnie's and introduced her to me. We started dating immediately. She was a perky cheerleader with short blonde hair. We got pretty serious, and I hated the thought of going back to Webster without her. The time for me to leave was getting close.

Mac was a big guy and had played college football. I was pretty strong, but he would let me hit him in the stomach as hard as I could. It didn't seem to phase him. He was a high school football official and one day he and I went down to Fayetteville for a state officials' meeting. We grilled each other on football rules all the way down. We were really close now and I told him about Bonnie and how I didn't want to leave her. We were even talking marriage for gosh sakes. Driving and marriage happen early in Arkansas. I don't think that Mac wanted me to leave either.

Mac had an idea. He took me over to Mountain Home and introduced me to the football coach. The coach said he could use a St. Louis kid on his team, and I could go to school there if I lived with Mac. Mac, Dorothy, Bonnie and I all thought it was a great idea, but when I called Mom to tell her the plan, and that I wasn't coming home, she quickly vetoed it and ordered me to come home on the next bus. I was pretty upset with her but I came home. No telling how my life would have turned out if Mom hadn't put her foot down. I was pretty sad when I left Mac, Dorothy and Bonnie, and I never saw any of them again. We wrote a lot for a while but as I found other interests at Principia my sights turned in another direction.

It seems like a lot of interesting stuff happed on Lake Norfork. To get across the lake from Henderson to Mountain Home you had to ride the ferry. I believe that in the last few years they built a bridge. Sometimes at night we would go down and fish for white bass off the ferry dock and watch the cars and people come and go. It was all pretty slow and peaceful. Sometimes it was busy. We were down there late one night when this guy pulled up to get on the ferry. We decided to quit fishing and just ride over and back.

Apparently the guy was drunk. He pulled his car up to the front edge of the ferry and stopped at the chain. On one side of the ferry was a red light on a post and on the other side a green light on a post. The guy didn't leave his car and sat there with the motor running. We guess that he dozed off for a second, and looked up and saw that green light. For some reason he put it in gear and drove right through the chain and off the front of the ferry. The ship's pilot stopped the boat immediately and may have thrown it in reverse. Anyway, the car slowly sank in about 100 feet of water with this guy clawing at the back window as it went down. It was a horrible sight. It took divers several days to retrieve the body. The car is still down there I guess.

The bus ride to the lake from St. Louis was a long one, and didn't take a direct route. The bus from St. Louis to West Plains was your normal Greyhound. The bus from West Plains down into Arkansas was smaller and the last "bus" over to Henderson was a beat up old station wagon. When I went down in 1953 I was the only passenger in the station wagon, so I sat up front with the driver. He was a pretty seedy old country boy. As we drove along the two lane highway a big old hound spotted us coming, and ran out into the road ahead of us. He was careful to stay on his side of the road. He barked and barked like a lot of country dogs do.

The driver did a curious thing. He mumbled under his breath that he was "sick and tired of that damn dog", and as we got closer he slowed down and slightly opened his door. Just as we were about to pass the unsuspecting dog, he threw the door open and knocked fido flat. As we sped down the road he looked into his rear view mirror and screamed, "I got the son of a bitch, I got the son of a bitch good!" I looked back with horror, and saw the dog sprawled on the road. I don't know if he was dead or just knocked cold. Either way, the guy made his point, and I didn't ask any questions.

E. UNCLE BUD'S

I believe it was the summer of 1950 after I finished the 8th grade that I went to work for my Uncle Bud Oberhaus in Union, Missouri. Uncle Bud owned a Western Auto store on the square and was moving into a bigger building across from the Franklin County Courthouse. I was to help with the move and work in the store. He paid me a little and gave me room and board with he and Aunt Verna, and my younger cousins MJ and Becky.

Dad drove me down there and took me and my stuff straight to the new building. They were still getting it ready for the move. Dad stood around and talked with Uncle Bud for a while and then he said he had to leave. "Before I go son, there is something I want to talk to you about", Dad said. "What is it?" I replied. "Lets go in this back room here". The suspense was building. "Look son, this is your first time away from home and I just want you to be sure to protect yourself." Dad had taught me how to box, and to fight, and I assured him I wouldn't forget what I learned. "That's not what I'm talking about." I didn't have a clue, and looked at him blankly. "What I'm trying to tell you son is to protect yourself, use a rubber."

I was a little slow but I finally figured it out. I promised him that I would be sure to use one. That was as close as Dad and I ever got to a discussion about the "birds and bees". I guess I was 13. I don't remember that I ever needed one that summer but I knew plenty of filling stations around town where you could get one for a quarter. I thought about buying one to carry around just in case, but I decided to save the quarter.

Uncle Bud worked me pretty hard. I worked a full 8 hour day and then I would go out at night with Bobby Keaney, a guy several years older than me who also worked for Uncle Bud. Bobby was 3 or more years older, but not much bigger than me. He was one of those small wiry guys. Bobby smoked and drank, and lived with his alcoholic mother in an apartment above a store downtown. I got introduced to a lot of wild stuff that summer.

Bobby and I got into a fight the first week I was there. It seems that he resented the bosses' nephew being around, and having to watch out for me. After we got that out of our system we were pretty good friends.

You may have heard of roadside "Honky-Tonks", well I was hanging around them quite a bit. Age didn't seem to matter. Some of those older gals seemed to get a kick out of teaching this young city kid how to dance and drink beer from a bottle. There were a lot of wild parties, and it seemed like everyone smoked and drank. Aunt Verna didn't have a clue about what I was doing, but she did worry a lot, and asked me a lot of questions.

I did a lot of good stuff too. I learned how to set up and stock a store, and eventually how to wait on customers and ring up the cash register. Sometimes Uncle Bud would take us home for lunch, but a lot of the time we would go out the back of the store and down the alley to the "White Rose Cafe". It was there that I was introduced to their specialty "brain sandwiches". The thought of eating a brain sandwich made me ill and I would never try it. Then one day I did eat a few bites, and it did make me sick. I don't recommend them. Hamburgers were fine. Who knew beef and grease and fried foods were so bad for you?

For the life of me I can't remember if I worked for Uncle Bud one or two summers. I think I worked there the summer of 1952 too. One thing that happened was that I met the "Allen twins". Viola and Iola were identical twins. My Dad would have said "they were well deformed". I learned how to tell them apart, and I started dating Iola. There is nothing quite like young summer love. Sometimes Iola made me as queasy as that brain sandwich. I didn't hang around with Bobby as much after Iola came on the scene.

We would go to movies, parties, and just hang out. We went to the river and swam a lot. You couldn't tell then apart in a bathing suit either. I learned that Iola had a very tiny spot in the corner of her eye.

Sometimes Viola would pretend to be Iola, and hug and kiss around. Of course, I acted dumb and surprised when she would confess, but I knew. Why not?

Aunt Verna really seemed concerned when she learned I had taken up with the twins. "Now Skipper (Skip was my nick name) you be careful around those Allen twins." I always wondered what she thought she knew. They really were good girls. At least with me. I remember one night being at a place on the river with Iola. We had been swimming all day and were hanging around this place to eat and dance. We walked out into the moonlight, and stood on a small bridge over the river. The juke box was playing "The Theme or Song From The Moulin Rouge", and the sound carried over the water and through the night. It was very romantic and very dramatic for a couple of young teenagers. That was the first real kiss I remember, and it seemed to last forever. Naturally that became our song. I was pretty sure I was in love.

Every Saturday night at the city park in Union they had what they called a "Picnic". It was held at the big dance pavilion in the center of the park. There was always a band, and the big dance was the "two-step". Iola and I almost always went to it.

Being the big city kid in town for the summer has its good and bad points. The girls always seem more interested but the boys get a little jealous. Some might be tempted to test you. Dad had worked hard to teach me how to fight, and for a brief time I had gone down to the St. Louis YMCA and worked with the Golden Gloves boxing program. I'll be right up front and tell you that I was no match for the other kids in the program. I got pounded pretty good most of the time, but I did learn how to look like a boxer, and I learned how to work a speed bag.

In fact I got pretty good at it, and would make one hum. I had my own bag set up in the basement at 548 Summit, and I took it with me, and set it up in Uncle Bud's basement in Union. I made sure those Union boys saw me work on it and let them know I was in the Golden Gloves. The bluff worked perfectly because they pretty much left me alone.

Except for one older guy who had dated Iola, and who resented my coming on the scene. He showed up drunk one night at a picnic with a bunch of his ugly friends. I figured I was going to have to either be brave and foolish or run like hell. Somehow the twins talked them into leaving and my cover was still safe.

Uncle Bud was quite a guy. He never drank anything but Stag Beer. There were a lot of small "corner bars" in Union and Washington, and he would take me with him. I'd have a soda, and he really would put salt and egg in his beer. Uncle Bud always had a boat of some kind. He would keep them on the Burbis River or the Missouri or the Gasconade. One time he took me out on the Missouri during a flood. I admit to being scared out of my wits. There were logs and trees and parts of houses floating out there. We shouldn't have been on the river at floodtide. Finally it happened. He ran over a log and tore the outboard motor right of the transom. We didn't sink but we took on water. Finally someone saw us and towed us in.

The last summer I stayed with Bud and Verna was 1957, the summer before I was married on August 30th, and before I started law school on September 3rd. I had a job working for Lee Young who was a lawyer and a CPA. He had offices in Union and Washington. We thought it would be good experience for me to work for a lawyer before I started law school. I would stay with them all week, then drive home to Webster on the weekends. I was 21, and Sharon and I were going through our pre-wedding jitters.

The problem with the law job was that Lee decided he could use me more on the accounting side rather than the law side, even though I had zero accounting experience or knowledge. I learned how to use an adding machine and got stuck doing a lot of boring office work for a while.

The Missouri Legislature had just passed a law that required all school districts to be audited. A lot of those small rural districts had never been audited. Lee chose me and one of his accountants to be his team on all the school audits he landed. That's what I did the rest of the summer. Neither Bill or I had any idea what the law required, so we just did our best. It was like the "blind leading the blind".

It was my first experience of power over other people, with the exception of my little brother Charles. These local school boards and administrators were scared to death of "the auditors". We would come to the school acting like we knew what we were doing, and would pretty much have them under our thumbs. You would be amazed at what poor records most of them had. Some were literally hundreds of receipts in a shoe box. Our job was not easy and we were constantly calling the school secretary in to explain this or that. I discovered that it is actually the school secretary that ran most of the schools.

I went to a lot of interesting towns and schools doing those audits. After a while we realized that not only did we not know how to audit, but we didn't know what kind of reports to write. We just muddled through. Near the end of the summer Lee sold his accounting offices to a big firm in St. Louis. I'll never forget the day that this Jewish CPA, a partner in the firm, whose name was Manney something, showed up at the school we were auditing. He spent a couple of hours reviewing what we were doing, decided it was all wrong, and fired Bill on the spot. I guess he fired me too, except I was supposed to have been on the law side. It didn't really matter because my summer was about to end anyway. Bill had a family.

It was hard on Sharon and me to be apart all week, and we tried to make up for it on the weekends. I had bought my first real car that summer so I could drive back and forth. Bud helped me pick it out at the Mercury dealer in Union. It was a beautiful lime green 1953 Mercury that could really fly. One early Monday morning I was headed for Union on the old Route 66 highway. I was really late and had a long way to go. Up ahead they were pulling cars over for a survey or something. I slowed down to get in line when something really dumb came over me. I realized that I just didn't have time to be bothered by whatever it was they wanted. So, instead of stopping, I hit the gas and flew on by. I didn't see the 3 Missouri Highway Patrol cars at first, but I sure saw them start to chase me.

I got up to about 100 mph pretty quick and had a good lead on them. Even so, I knew eventually they would catch me if I stayed on 66. There was an old motel at the intersection of 66 and Lindberg so I wheeled in behind the restaurant there. Almost immediately the 3 patrol cars whizzed by with sirens and lights blazing. My heart was about to jump out of my chest. For some lucky reason no one got my license number. I decided to go over to highway 50 or Manchester into Washington on the old highway. Needless to say, I was very late but much wiser.

F. ORCHIDS, SURVEY STAKES, WAREHOUSES, ROOFING AND GUARDING

Like most kids I had a wide array of summer jobs growing up. I've already mentioned working in my uncle's Western Auto Store, at a lake resort and as an "auditor". But there were more. In the summer of 1951, after my Freshman year, I got a job at Nettie's Greenhouse in Kirkwood. I would take the bus or hitchhike out there each day. This is where they grew the orchids that they sold in their St. Louis flower shops. They taught me how to pot orchids, water orchids, feed orchids and just about anything else involved in growing the darn things. We had thousands of them. You had to do it right. They were very delicate. I was by far the youngest employee. I was just 15.

I did a pretty good job although there were those moments when I would water a fellow worker rather then the flowers. Goofing off came pretty natural to me and sometimes I had to learn the consequences. To me the job was summer fun and a way to get some money. It was a lot more to my employers. I didn't really understand that until I became an employer myself and hired a few goof offs of my own. "What goes around..."

In 1952 I worked for Uncle Bud again, and in 1953 I got a job in the Western Auto Warehouse in St. Louis. I had to join the union so I became a Teamster with the CIO and AFL. This was pretty hard work and got me ready for my senior year of football in the Fall. I spent a lot of time on the dock unloading freight cars. Sometimes it would be over 110 degrees in those boxcars. For a few weeks they put me on the night shift as an order filler in the basement of the warehouse. There weren't very many of us around and that great big place got pretty spooky. It was a hot St. Louis summer, but we were filling store orders for Christmas. That seemed weird.

The problem with our night crew was that everyone was a goof-off, including the supervisor. We played with the toys and games, hid from one another among the thousands of boxes stacked to the ceiling, and sometimes played demolition derby with the fork lift trucks used by the day shift. That all ended when someone ran a fork through the side of a deep freezer. One night another supervisor showed up and fired everyone but me. I had connections because my Dad was high up in Western Auto. They put me back in the sun unloading boxcars. One night right before everyone got fired, a guy attacked me with a pencil and jabbed it into my right forearm. You can still see the pencil lead embedded in my arm to this day.

After I graduated from Principia in June of 1954, and after my trip to Kansas with Ginger, I came home and went to work with

Rowland Engineering Company, out of Clayton. Bob Smith lived next door and ran one of their survey crews. They put me to work doing the hard labor. I had to do a lot of digging, and I cleared a lot of brush so we could run or shoot our survey lines. We did namely big commercial or subdivision jobs. Eventually I even learned how to work most of the surveying instruments, but all that is forgotten now.

My worst experience as a surveyor happened when I spent most of one day with a machete cutting a sight line. It was hot and apparently most of what I cut through was poison oak and poison ivy. It didn't help that I had my shirt off and got a sunburn on top of it. That was the most miserable I ever remember being. I was one big gooey blister from the waist up. I was in a medicated type plaster cast and couldn't really move my arms. I missed a lot of work. Sharon and I had started dating and that was a lot of fun. I was in no condition to make any moves.

When I was at home in Webster for the summer from Drury College in 1955 and 1956 I worked for Carr Brothers Roofing Company. John and Ralph Carr. It was hard work and pretty good pay, but not something I wanted to do for a life time. In fact, my experience as a roofer, probably had more to do with my finally getting serious about my education than all the advice and lectures so many had given to me.

When I started with them I was a "shingle carrier". It's a lot like the old "hod carrier" for bricklayers and Masons. Today a truck full of shingles pulls up to the house and a conveyor belt type machine puts the shingles on the roof for the roofers. In my day, there was no such thing, and I had to carry each bundle, on my shoulder, up a ladder and across the roof. It was hard and it was dangerous. Fortunately I was young, strong and athletic. I survived.

I didn't think I would survive that first day. It had rained the night before, and everything at the construction site was wet and muddy. Unfortunately, that first house was not a one story ranch. This job was in Ladue, a very rich part of St. Louis County. The house was a huge two and a half story frame with lots of dormers and valleys. The shingles were better than most and so thicker and heavier. They were piled up in the mud. Each bundle weighed about 75 pounds. The card board that sort of held them together was soaked and torn so that they wiggled and wobbled each time I put a bundle on my shoulder.

The crew chief explained what my job was and showed me how to grab a bundle, heave it over my shoulder, and walk up the ladder. (He didn't actually walk up it himself). Here's the problem. The old wood extension ladder was stretched out as far as it could go, and leaning up against the edge of the roof. The roofers were already on the roof putting down a primary layer of black felt paper. They were about ready for some shingles.

I hoisted the first bundle to my shoulder. Immediately water and roof granules went all over me. The bundle tore and wiggled and flopped uncontrollably as I walked to the ladder. My feet sunk in the mud from my weight and the weight of the shingles. When I got to the ladder I steadied myself and put one, cautious and muddy foot on the bottom rung. I looked up, my hat hit the bundle and fell off into the mud. It looked like a mile to the top of the ladder. I tried to climb the ladder with both muddy feet trying to slip and throw me off. The weight of the bundle would shift and try to throw me. Slowly I climbed toward the top. When I got half way the ladder bowed in so I was almost upside down.

When I finally got to the top I looked down. That was a mistake. Never look down! Now I had to actually step off the ladder onto a steep roof with muddy shoes and a wobbly bundle of shingles. I literally froze. I couldn't move. By now the bundle was cutting into my shoulder and felt like it weighed 200 pounds. One of the roofers saw my plight and sort of talked me through it.

I should have quit then and there. Any sane person would have. But I was determined I could do it and I did. It was one of the longest days of my life. I could have been killed. Both summers were hard, but nothing like that first day.

Roofing didn't seem to attract the highest caliber of people. At least not Carr Brothers. Several of my fellow workers resented my education and never referred to me by name. I was always "college boy". One guy in particular seemed to try to put me down. College Boy would sort of slur and drip off his lips. For the most part I would just ignore all this and just make the best of it.

The work was hard and the heat unbearable. It could easily be 120 degrees on a roof and the material and tools so hot you couldn't touch them without getting burned. When it got real hot we started at 6 a.m. I was a shingle carrier the summer of '55 but a full blown roofer the summer of '56. You wore an apron or a nail pouch, and instead of a hammer you used a roofing hatchet. The hatchet side was used mainly to deftly swing at a bundle of shingle and cut or break the wire holding the bundle together without cutting the shingles. The hatchet also had a gauge on it that you used to keep the shingles even so you would have a straight row and not a crooked one.

The blunt side of the hatchet was larger than a hammer head so there would be less chance of missing the flat headed roofing nails. Today, most roofs are put on with staple guns. We old timers were like John Henry trying to outwork the steam shovel or any other new fangled contraption. The secret was to stand with your feet a foot or so apart, and with loose shingles piled on top your shoes, bend from the waist, and hammer and measure each one into place. A good roofer would have a staccato cadence to his hammering and would almost sound like a machine as he worked his way across the roof, one layer at a time.

One day I had had enough of this doofus calling me college boy and I told him so. Unfortunately, we were on a roof at the time and he came after me with his roofing hatchet. You should have seen this college boy run around that roof. Finally, the other guys got him under control and Ralph said he would fire him if he ever did anything like that again. Vernon never bothered me after that, and the summer was about over any way.

Being a shingle carrier the summer of '55 got me in such good shape that I was hard as nails. I came back to Springfield for a Sig Ep summer rush party at the fraternity house at 1035 N. Jefferson. I'm sure the party was illegal and I know the beer and poker were. We were all down in the basement rec room and two of the rushees were feeling sick so I took them out front for some fresh night air. One of them was a scrawny kid named Vernon Chase.

The 3 of us were minding our own business when these two guys walked by and up our front walk. They were obviously drunk. For no apparent reason, the big guy hit Vernon right in the face, and knocked him up into a pillar. I guess my paternal instinct took over and I felt responsible for this rushee. I jumped on this guy and he and I rolled around in the grass. He was a bull of a guy and kept trying to gouge my eyes out. I got a hammer lock on his head and was pounding him in the face over and over with no apparent affect. Everybody heard the commotion and rushed out of the house and broke it up. They left and I was a hero. I really believe it was that roofing job that saved me. Vernon was still out.

A post script to the story was that this guy was a local gang leader and weight lifter and might have killed me if he hadn't been drunk.

He saw me once in Fishers Hi Boy on St. Louis Street. He looked at me like he ought to know me, but then gave up and went on. I didn't remind him and was very relieved.

I started law school at St. Louis University after the summer of '57 and after working for Lee Young. During school I had a job at the St. Louis County Probate Court in Clayton and just worked there full time the summer of 1958. Near the end of my second year in law school, my good friend Henry Luepke asked me where I was going to work, and suggested that I apply for a plant guard job at the Chevrolet Plant where he always worked. So I did. I got the job, but Hank didn't get hired back. Said they couldn't get a uniform big enough to fit his 6'8" frame. Hank was pretty nice about it, but a little upset.

It was a great job and great pay. Best of all I got to wear a uniform and a badge. I felt as proud as Barney Fife working for old Andy.

The Chevrolet plant in St. Louis was a huge place with thousands of employees. It was surrounded by a high chain link and barbwire fence. Security worked both ways. First to keep those outside from getting in, and second to keep the employees from stealing the company blind. That was the job of the plant guards. We were considered part of management. The plant ran two shifts, but we ran three. If you worked the day shift you got the base pay, a little more for the 12 midnight to 8 a.m. "graveyard" shift. The three months I was there I worked each shift. You also got double time for holidays and weekends. I worked all the holidays and weekends. I had never made so much money. It took me several years as a lawyer to make as much as I made in one summer as a plant guard. I was tempted to stay on permanently.

I soon learned that the plant employees hated the guard. We were always snooping around and spying on them. During the day shift I did several different things. I was the last one to check a newly made Chevrolet out of the back gate to be picked up by Auto Transport to be trucked to a dealership. A driver would drive the new car off the assembly line and to my gate. I would check all the paperwork, make sure it had a cigarette lighter, and also make sure some employee wasn't trying to smuggle something out in the car. You can't believe how fast those cars came off that assembly line.

There was a tall watch tower in the middle of the yard behind the plant. It was all like a busy small city. There were streets and railroad tracks criss-crossing from every direction. We observed all of this from the tower and actually controlled lights and switches at the crossing. It was a good place to spy on everyone from, and to check for problems and accidents. Sometimes those cars would be in a wreck 30 seconds after they came off the line.

The other job I had on the day and night shift was to check the employees out of the plant at various gates at quitting time. They had to open their lunch boxes etc., for inspection, and we would pat down any suspicious bulges in their clothes. I really got some looks that would kill doing that.

The employees had locker rooms and showers they could use to change in if they wanted to. We would climb out on the roof and spy from the skylight to try to catch them hiding something in their clothes. They would steal tools and auto parts. One guy stole a whole motor, piece by piece, by tossing it out a window at night and over the fence in the grass. He would pick up the piece when he got off work. Wrenches and screwdrivers would be tied to their legs. They were clever.

You can't imagine how noisy and busy that plant was the first two shifts, and how eerily quiet it was on the graveyard shift. Not many lights were left on. There were a lot of dark spots and shadows. Now our attention formed on threats from the outside. People would hide in boxcars coming into the plant and try to get in that way. They would climb the fence. The tower watch on that shift was pretty boring and I had a lot of trouble staying awake. We would have to walk a beat through the plant and punch in at various points along the way. I didn't know that all this was being monitored by our control headquarters. One night I was tired and pretty spooked by the darkness and danger of the Corvette plant. I didn't like slowly walking alone in there, jumping at every sight and sound. So I got the bright idea of running from station to station, get the whole hour round over within 10 minutes, and just hunker down until it was time to start the next round.

I guess they went nuts in the office because my station lights were going on like a Christmas tree. It didn't take very long for my sergeant to show up and ask me what the hell I was doing? From then on I did the beat right, and carried one enormous night stick and a flashlight. Finally, the summer was over and so was the last summer job I ever had. It was back to the law books for one last year and then out into the real world of work. That world went from July 1960 until October, 1997 when I retired from the law. I still miss those summers. Life hasn't been the same since.

1985. Charles and Ted at Uncle Bud's cabin, Gasconade River.

CHAPTER FIFTEEN

SEMPER FI

•My Life As A Marine•

I have no war stories to tell or acts of heroism to relate. I might not mention my experience as a Marine at all except that it is a part of me, and occupied 6 years of my life. The Korean War was over when a truce was signed in July of 1953. I had been too young for that war. My Dad had been too old for World War II. The draft was still in effect but I was probably deferred as long as I was in college.

One night Charlie Crabtree, a fraternity brother, and I were out drinking Kool-Aid with a Marine recruiter and John Sherman a Marine captain we knew and also a Sig Ep. We were 19 years old and starting our second year at Drury. The next thing I knew they had us both enlisted, and I officially joined on November 17, 1955. I signed up for 6 years to November 17, 1961. My service No. was 1537505. I will probably never forget it because if any officer or non com asked you your number you had better know it, or else.

Why did we do it? Well, one reason is we were pressured and under the influence of Kool-Aid. But it seemed like a good deal at the time. They had a special for college students where you didn't have to go on active duty, and could fulfill your military obligation in the reserves. There was a Marine Reserve unit right on the Drury campus, the 12th Rifle Company. I immediately started attending drills one night a week. Occasionally we would drill for a whole weekend. Each summer we were required to go to summer camp for two weeks. I made a lot of interesting friends and Charlie and I had some wild experiences.

The summer of 1956 was my first summer camp. We flew to Camp Pendleton, California. It was a mini boot camp. Fortunately by then I had a pretty good idea what was going on, and I was always in good shape. I qualified expert on the rifle range with my M-1 rifle. We crawled through mud and obstacle courses, played war games (just like being a kid again), and did all the normal training a Marine goes through. The regular Marine DIs particularly wanted a piece of we reservists.

There are a lot of rattlesnakes at Camp Pendleton. You had to be careful crawling around out there. One day on the live fire machine gun range, one of our boys came face to face with a rattler, forgot what was going on, and was killed by the machine gun fire when he jumped up.

It seems like we went to several different Marine bases for summer camp. Camp Pendleton, Pickle Meadows for winter training, 29 Palms for desert warfare training, and Camp Coronado for amphibious training. The only bright spot about summer camp was that you got the weekend in between off. We always had wild adventures in California, Mexico or Nevada. I can't remember most of them and can't tell the others. Lets just say "Marines will be Marines".

The weekend in Las Vegas in 1961 was interesting. A few of us had chartered a bus to take us there and back from 29 Palms. We sold seats on the bus and were responsible to get everyone back to camp. When we got to Vegas each person was responsible to get himself back to the bus pickup spot on Sunday night. We had to do a good bit of rounding up to get everybody on board. We were missing a guy named Webster, who I figured might be trouble. We couldn't find him, so I had the driver go over to the police station. I was in my first year of practicing law now, and I had to talk hard to get them to release him into my custody. He had been drunk and disorderly. He had been thrown in jail about 2 hours after we hit town on Friday night.

Camp Coronado is in San Diego near the Mexican border. A bunch of us decided to go to Tijuana for the evening. On a bridge crossing into the city we got in a brief fight with some sailors. Marines and sailors traditionally don't get along. Then we began to hit one establishment after another. We vowed to stay together because Tijuana was not safe, and you were better off in a group. We decided it was time to leave, and we had lost one of the guys. We began to panic in an effort to find him. He could be killed or never seen again. I remember running into bars etc., almost knocking people down trying to find him. Finally we found him in some bath room with this Mexican girl. He complained that he wasn't finished, but we got him out of there anyway.

We caught a bus back to the camp, and it was about 4 a.m. Our commanding officer, Major Bill Cantrell, was just getting up, and headed for the head to shave. We almost walked right into him. He realized that we had been up all night and hadn't slept. We saluted and he assured us that we four would be the first off the "towers" that day. We made it to our barracks just as revelry was playing.

After breakfast they took us to one of the base swimming pools. The pool was manned by burly marine life guards and instructors. There was the "tower" at the deep end of the pool, all forty feet of it. They were going to train us how to jump off the side of a ship should that ever become necessary in combat. As promised, Major Cantrell suggested to the DI in charge that we four boys would be first. We were not yet recovered from the night's activities, so that climb up the tower was no picnic. When we got to the top I got dizzy and queasy just looking down. That huge pool now looked like a bath tub, and I was sure I would miss it.

The pool marines at the top told us to cup one hand around our private parts, and the other under our chin, and jump. This was to prevent them from being torn off or smashed when we hit the water. I can't stand heights that much, and as I stood on the edge looking down, I explained to this fellow that I didn't really want to do it. He showed me a lot of sympathy by sticking his foot in my back and pushing me off. I can still hear my cry of agony as I fell for what seemed like an eternity. I hit. I was alive. Everything was still intact and attached. When I came out of the pool the major asked me if I wanted to go again. "With all due respect sir, no thank you!"

For most of my Marine Corp experience I was a private. I finally got promoted to Lance Corporal. At one summer camp I was the NCO on duty. I was in charge of our barracks for the evening while everybody was out having fun on base at the base bars called "slop chutes". The guys began to straggle back in and go to bed. Several of the really late arrivals were pretty drunk and wanted to fight me. They were also getting sick. It was quite a scene as I put one after the other in the showers. They were throwing up and some trying to fight me to get out. I had 4 guys in there, and it was quite a scene, and quite a mess. Of course, I knew that it was easier to clean them up and sober them up in the shower than in their bunks or the barracks.

When I was in St. Louis going to law school for three years I transferred to the St. Louis unit, the Third Infantry Battalion. In 1956 and the following years the United States and its allies were involved with problems in the Middle East. Egypt had sunk ships in the Suez Canal and blocked vital shipping. There was a crisis in Beirut. The Marines were called in, including our Marine Reserve Unit. I believe that it was 1958 when we had boarded a plane with full battle gear to take us to the Middle East. I could see my life and my future going up in smoke. Suddenly the engines of the plane stopped and an outside door opened. A Colonel entered and informed us that our orders had been cancelled and we weren't going after all.

Loud cheers went up from all over the plane except for this regular Marine sergeant who was seated next to me. He couldn't believe it and was very upset. He started screaming, "No, No, I want to kill some A-RABS, I want to kill some A-RABS!! " I got out of there as quick as I could.

My life as a Lance Corporal didn't last long. The last summer camp I attended we were practicing crawling on our belly with a rifle and pack before going through a live fire course. This one DI was being a particular jerk, and hitting people with his swagger stick. He finally was over me screaming about what a lousy Marine I was and hit me several times in the helmet and legs. I snapped. I jumped to my feet and went after him. They restrained me and shortly thereafter I was a private again. It ended as it began.

I'm not aware of any other Marines in our family except for my brother Charles. He joined up about the time I got out. I'm sure that he has his own stories to tell. All in all, my Marine experience was a good one. I have come to respect and appreciate the sacrifice so many have made to keep us safe and keep us free.

Ted at Camp Pendleton, California-1956

Ted, center, during helicopter assault training, 1957- Camp Coronado, San Diego.

CHAPTER SIXTEEN

•Family•

I have been blessed with a wonderful family. There is so much that I would like to say about each of them. Their contributions to my life are scattered throughout this book. What follows is a brief account of my immediate family.

My dad was Theodore Clifton Salveter, Jr. He was born on April 11, 1909 in Lincoln, Nebraska. He died in Springfield, Missouri on July 9, 1995 at the age of 86. Dad was truly a unique and interesting character. He was a big guy for most of his life and a good athlete. He weighed about 235 pounds, and was 5' 11" when he played football at Missouri University. He had played football and baseball at Webster Groves. He hated to lose, and never cut you any slack. He became upset when his grandchildren beat him at tennis or cards.

Dad had a golden gift of gab. He was a salesman most of his life. He could tell a story or joke about any subject. He never forgot one.

Even in the nursing home he remembered them right up to the end. He had a lot of unique sayings that he would quote, that always seemed appropriate for the moment or problem at hand. He quoted "Ole the Swede" a lot for advice. Dad was not perfect, he made a lot of mistakes. Some say he wasn't a good role model. Maybe so, but nevertheless I miss him. I've never known anyone quite like him.

My mom was Nelda Marie Anna Oberhaus Salveter. "Girlie" to her family. She was born on October 10, 1915 in Washington, Missouri and died June 30, 1983 in Springfield, Missouri. She was 67 and died from colon cancer. She was the best person I ever knew. She deserved better than she got.

She grew up in Washington, Missouri, and because she was good in track was dubbed "The fastest girl in Franklin County". She always winced at the double meaning of that title. That's probably what got Dad's attention. She was fast. I remember racing her out on Summit in front of our house in Webster. In street shoes, and no warm up, she could still beat me. I hated it then. Now I can appreciate it and laugh.

What I remember about mom, and what people remember about her was her unconditional love for all, and her ability to see some good in everyone. She touched the lives of all she met, whether it was as a saleslady at Lammert's Department Store, Bascombs or The Station in Webster. Her church was The First Church of Christ

Scientist in Webster. She was in some ways a simple, uncomplicated and not educated beyond high school woman. But behind that was a person of great wisdom and insight.

Mom had one problem that gave us many laughs. She didn't always say what she meant. Like the time we were celebrating the 4th of July at Charles'. It was a beautiful evening, and as we sat there watching the kids shoot off their fireworks she said "Oh, I'm so delightful". She took all the kidding in stride, and the insistence of her grandchildren to take out her false teeth and show them. A guy couldn't have had a better mom. She left too soon.

God blessed me with a wonderful life partner. She and I had three great kids, and weathered many of life's storms together. Sharon Lee Downen and I were married on August 30, 1957, just a few days before I started law school. It was a lot for a guy to take on all at once, but it has all worked out pretty darn well!

After that infamous first date on New Years Eve 1953, we didn't date again until the summer of 1954. Things got serious pretty quick, and when I went off to Drury in the Fall I hated to leave her behind. I believe that we wrote almost every day. She followed me to Drury the next year, and we were "pinned". We were engaged in November, 1956 at the Sig Ep Founder's Day Formal. She has often complained (half seriously) that I roped and branded her too soon. I always remind her that she's the one who chased me.

Sharon has three fairly important attributes a guy looks for in a girl. She is very smart, attended Drury, graduated with a degree in Education from Washington University and a Masters in Education from S.M.S.U. She taught at Valley Park and Pattonville while I was in law school, and was an E.S.L. teacher at Jarrett and Hickory Hills Middle Schools until she retired in June 1997. She has a great personality and is a lot of fun to be with either in a group or just the two of us. Last but not least she is very pretty, and has stayed in good shape through diet and exercise, and by being married to me. She is a good and spiritual person, and has served as my conscience all these years. Not a bad package.

We don't look forward to old age, but here we are already. We do look forward to growing old together. We've survived and enjoyed forty-eight years of marriage. We took "for better or worse, in good times and bad" seriously. I admit that we had some serious second thoughts before we said "I do". I didn't know she was having any at the time. I guess everybody does. The summer of 1957 was hot, and as I spent each week in Union away from Sharon, I had plenty of time to think about the wedding day ahead. I had some serious cold sweats. I was just 21, she was still 19. Were we crazy? At the rehearsal I almost freaked out. When the wedding started, and I was waiting off the sanctuary there in the Webster Groves Baptist Church with Jim Singer my best man and the others, I looked at that side door, and almost went out it. I'm glad I didn't. I would have missed a lot.

I would have missed that simple honeymoon where we drove all the way out Lindberg to a Howard Johnson's and stayed there till school started. Of course, we didn't go straight to the motel as I had planned. She said she was hungry, and we had to stop at a restaurant. I think she was just scared. I hope the best is yet to come.

When I was a senior in law school, Sharon and I agreed it was time to start our family. After all, I would be graduating and making lots of money as a lawyer. That turned out not to be true as I started work for the vast sum of $350.00 per month. Teddy was born on October 25, 1960 in St. John's Hospital. Our discussion etc, to start a family must have occurred on or about January 25, 1960.

Theodore Clifton Salveter, IV turned out to be an okay kid. I was very proud when my first born son came into my life. He seemed so little and helpless, a far cry from the man he has become. All parents tend to brag on their kids, but I truly have every right to brag about mine. Teddy is very smart. he went to Sunshine, Roundtree, Parkview, University of Missouri at Rolla and M.U. at Columbia. He got a geological engineering degree in 1983 and almost completed his masters in environmental engineering. He has worked for the Department of Pollution and Ecology in the State of Arkansas and for McClaren Hart Consulting Engineers. He has his P.E., and is currently the Environmental Engineer for City Utilities.

I admit that he has that superior air that all math and science guys have over we mere liberal arts majors. I remember one Christmas vacation when Teddy was home from Rolla and Tony from William Jewell. The boys and I were watching a basketball game on TV, and Tony proudly showed us his grades which were all A's as usual. Teddy looked at them and calmly said; "Not bad little brother, but why don't you come up to Rolla and take some real classes?" Tony had no reply, neither did I.

In October, 1986 Teddy and I went on a backpacking trip to the Smokey Mountains for 8 days. It was great to be alone with him in that beautiful place. I learned how strong and independent he is. He learned that his dad was old enough that I couldn't make it without him. Teddy played football, basketball and tennis at Parkview and even wrestled one year. He has many talents.

Teddy married Lisa in January of 1990. He adopted her daughter, Rachael, who was born on June 20, 1983, and they had one son, Brennon Anthony Salveter who was born June 14, 1991. He should have been the "V", but that didn't happen. His middle name is after his uncle Tony. We have two beautiful grandchildren.

On May 1, 1963 Philip Anthony Salveter was born. I have previously mentioned in this book that he died as a result of an auto accident on March 6, 1990. I also wrote a book about him in 1997 entitled "His Wonderful Life". Tony never married, and had no children that we know about. He grew up in Springfield, and attended Roundtree, Jarret and Parkview. He has degrees in Psychology and Business from William Jewel in 1985 and a J.D. from Missouri University School of Law in 1988. He was practicing law in Kansas City with Shook, Hardy and Bacon at the time of his death.

The most amazing thing about Tony, besides his intellect, was his terrific love for life, and for other people. He packed an enormous amount of living into his almost 27 years. My grief over his death has been almost unbearable at times. It is a life crisis that Sharon and I have borne together, and that has caused us to lean on each other for support. I doubt that I will ever recover.

I miss the phone calls, the occasional letters, that friendly "Hi Pop, just wanted to see how you were doing". The anticipation of his coming home, and the thrill of his car coming up the drive. Those warm bear hugs from a boy who had outgrown his dad. I miss our one on one basketball games, tennis, and our mutual infatuation with sports and the Mizzou Tigers, the Chiefs, the Cardinals and the Royals. I even miss the way he could con me into doing almost anything.

Sharon and I had planned a family of two, but to our surprise and amazement along came Paige Allison Salveter on January 6, 1967. She altered my life and continues to do so. She is the cause of great joy and a little frustration. Like her brothers, she is very smart, but very much a hands on people person. She also went to Roundtree, Jarrett and Parkview. She was the No. 1 tennis singles player for Parkview, and was Homecoming Queen her senior year. She was a Vikette, a cheerleader and a basketball player. She was also a wonderful singer and got many 1s at state.

She received a music and tennis scholarship from William Jewell and graduated in 1989 with a degree in Recreational Therapy. At Jewell she played No. 1 singles and won the Heart of America Conference 2 of the 4 years. She also plays the piano and the flute.

She married Dan Cotta on June 18, 1994 and they had no children. Dan was a Webster boy too. Paige also has a degree in Therapeutic Recreation from S.M.S.U. and a Masters in Education, and a Masters in Business Administration from Webster University. In her junior year in college she attended Harlaxton College at Grantham England. England and Europe have never been the same. She has worked for Charter Mental Hospital in Austin, Texas, Epworth Children's Home in Webster, was the activities director for Webster Hills Methodist Church, for Nestle-Purina in marketing, and Geoff Howe a British advertising agency. We enjoy long walks, tennis and just hanging out. Her moving to the Webster - St. Louis area had allowed me to vicariously return home. She moved to Kansas City when she married Andy Brez in February, 2005. He is now my favorite son in law! I now have two new "grandchildren", Cody and Sophie Brez. They are a delight.

Both Ted and Paige were unhappy with us for selling their old home place at 1635 E. Delmar. We had purchased the home in 1973 from Mrs. Umbarger who with her deceased husband Dr. Umbarger had built the place in 1917. We sold it and moved to 5173 S. Virginia Ave. on February 2, 2000. The children and family had a right to be upset. This place was part of the family, and there are many wonderful memories. The tennis court, pool, basketball court etc. Paige had her wedding reception there with a tent over the court, just like in the movies. If I had it to do over again I would not have sold the place. One of Tony's life long friends, Debbie Mallonee Shantz bought it, and it is in good hands.

We had a family farm of sorts down near Riverside in Christian County. Charles and his family lived there. I had two different big tree houses and a cabin that I had built myself. We bought it around 1963. A lot of great stuff happened there. Eventually we sold it to Johnnie Morris who owns the Bass Pro Shops. This was probably in the 90s. Charles bought a 400 acre farm near Halltown on Billie's Creek, and lives there now. I have been out of the tree house business for quite some time.

I have a half sister, Celia Marie Salveter who lives in Arlington, Texas. She was born on April 11, 1954 in St. Louis, Missouri. I have a half brother, Robert Salveter who is retired from the air force. He lives in Laughlin, Nevada. He was born on August 9, 1956 in Aledo, Illinois. Neither ever had any children. My dad had remarried after he and mom divorced. Mom never did remarry, but devoted the rest of her life to her two boys and her grandchildren.

My best friend aside from Sharon, and the person who has known me since the age of 5, is my brother Charles. He was born Charles Robert Salveter on February 16, 1941. We were still on the farm at Gray Summitt when he came along. He shares my memories and fascination with 548 Summit, with our mom and dad, and so many things. We've had our differences, and our lives have taken different turns, but down deep there is a very, very strong bond and love. When dad died in 1995 we were the only ones left who remembered how things were. I wish us both long life.

He was also born in St. Francis Hospital in Washington, Missouri. Doc Mays delivered us both. Unlike me, Charles didn't go from school to school. He started kindergarten at Lockwood in Webster, and right on to junior high and graduated from Webster high in 1959 along with Sharon's sister Mary. He attended Drury and got his bachelors and masters from S.M.S.U. He retired as Regional director of Vocational Rehabilitation, and now is the director of Lakes Country Rehabilitation. He has two daughters, Amy and Lara, both who have not yet married and have no children.

Charles has been a special uncle to my three kids. They all love their "Uncle Barley". If something, ever happened to Sharon, I imagine that I would move to the farm and live with Charles. We could talk about the old days in front of the fire and fall asleep in our chairs. But I'm not ready for that rocker yet!

I was especially spoiled by my paternal grandparents, and so they are very dear to my heart. I want to briefly mention them here.

My paternal grandparents, Theodore and Mae Salveter Sr., I remember as being very refined and solid people. They doted on me as the oldest grandchild and namesake. They desired to see that I did things right, and that I had good moral and ethical values. Being with them was always partly educational. They wanted to be sure that I spoke correctly and "to enunciate"! Grandpa Salveter would not tolerate slurring or soft-spoken speech. "Speak up", "enunciate", "speak distinctly" and "speak correctly". Manners were important. I needed to know the right fork or spoon to use. To say "thank you" and "please", and to look people in the eye, and give them a firm gripped handshake.

When I spent the night with them, which was one of my favorite things to do, we would always discuss God and His place in my life. When he would tuck me in grandpa and I would always recite.

"Today has been and yesterday and still I stand

the stronger for their passing.

Tomorrow I shall meet the day,

confident that God always has met and always

will meet every human need."

They taught me how to play cribbage, canasta, pinochle and a host of games. Before bed we would always have "black cows" (coke and ice cream) and grandma just straight chocolate ice cream. They loved to take me out to eat. Grandpa always thought that one day he'd like to own a restaurant. He never did. They liked to go downtown to Mrs. Hullings Cafeteria. It did have great food. At Christmas time they always gave great gifts, and the family dinner at their house was always special.

I would like to be a grandfather like that, but times seem to have changed. The kids are much too busy, and like Rodney Dangerfield, we "just don't get no respect". That's not entirely true. After all, they do endure my boring stories, and sometimes I think they actually like them.

My maternal grandparents were Henry and Christina Oberhaus of Washington, Missouri. As far as I know she never worked, but grandpa Oberhaus had a shoe shop and they lived up above it. Mom had three brothers, Lester, Raymond and Bud Oberhaus. They all stayed in the

Washington, Union area until their death.

Grandpa and Grandma Salveter, 1938.

Grandparents Henry and Christina Oberhaus, 1937.

Cave at farm near Riverside, 1988, Ted IV., Ted III., Tony and Charles Salveter.

1635 E. Delmar, 1991.

Ted, Rachael, and Brennon-1992.

Family Doubles- Ted, Sharon, Ted IV, and Paige Salveter.

1959- Charles, Mom, and Ted.

CHAPTER SEVENTEEN

•What's Next?•

W hen I started this project I had no idea that it would go on so long. "Amen", says the reader. Nevertheless, I'm glad that I did it. I feel like I have only scratched the surface, but how do you end one of these things? I guess you end it by looking to the future. The things I thought I would do when I retired, never got done. Like teaching law or political science at Drury or Missouri State, Little Theatre shows, running for political office again. I taught Business Law and Political Science classes at Drury University and Missouri State off and on from 1961 up to around 1985. I learned a lot from teaching, and I really enjoyed it. If I had it all to do over again I would give serious consideration to teaching in some college somewhere. I also taught the Pioneer Class at University Heights Baptist Church for over 30 years. You learn a lot more from teaching a class than taking one. I taught some classes in the Marine Corps too. Being a college guy and all. I don't seem to have any more time for those things now than I did before retirement. Where does the time go each day? Truthfully I believe that the simple things of life, taken one day at a time are really the best. As we age we should realize that the old ego doesn't need so much care and feeding. An old man once told me that someday I would come to know that the best thing that can happen to you each day is a good bowel movement. Think about it!

I am extremely curious about how things will turn out. We have declared war on "Terrorism". People are shooting and blowing each other up all over the world. We have started a necessary war in Afghanistan, and an unnecessary and costly war in Iraq. Can we beat terrorism? Will the Chiefs or Rams ever get to the Super Bowl again? So many things to think and worry about.

But what's next for me? I hope to see my grandchildren graduate from college. Maybe even medical or law school. I'd like to break 80 regularly. Some days I am happy when I break 90. I want my knees to last a while longer.

When I started this book so many years ago I wondered then if writing it would help me discover who I am. I think that it has. I am an ordinary guy who for a lot of his life, took most of what was going on around him for granted. I remember the moments, but somehow I feel like I wasn't always completely there. I would love to go back, and do it all over again. I don't take people and circumstances for granted much anymore. I know that nothing is guaranteed, and "that we may never pass this way again". Life can change in a heartbeat. So I can plan for my future, but when Tony died I learned that "Life is what happens while you are making other plans". Being an accidental lawyer hasn't turned out so bad. All the same, this book has turned out to be more of a project than I realized. I feel like that guy who was tarred and feathered, and being run out of town on a rail. His thought was that "If it weren't for the honor of the thing he'd just as soon not do it". Whatever is next for me, I hope that you are a part of it. I hope we are both in our "rightful place"! If you want to know how my story ended, you will have to ask someone who was there. Chances are I won't be around.

ABOUT THE AUTHOR

Ted C. Salveter, III. is a retired lawyer living in Springfield, Missouri. He grew up in St. Louis in the 40s and 5Os in Webster Groves. He holds a degree in Psychology with a Minor in English from Drury University, and a J.D. from St. Louis University School of Law. He has taught law and political science at Drury and Missouri State University. He was elected to the Springfield School Board and the Missouri Legislature. His only other book was "His Wonderful Life" about his son Tony who died in 1990.

CPSIA information can be obtained at www.ICGtesting.com
Printed in the USA
LVOW07s0244130415

434318LV00001B/290/P